POETRY

BURIED

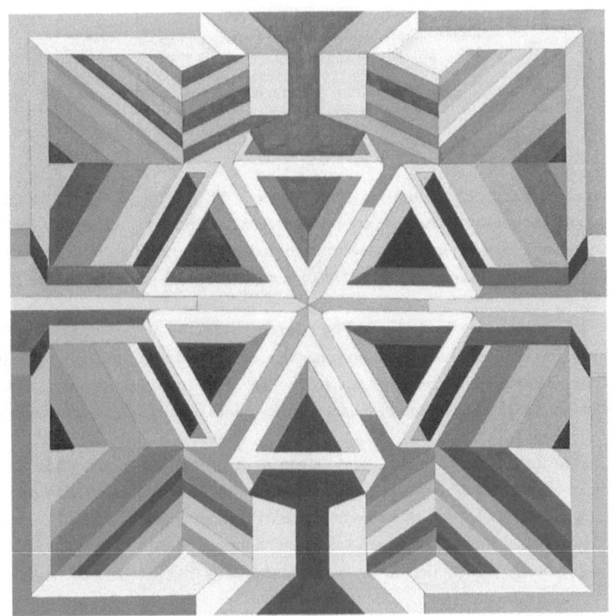

IN

GEOMETRY

SELECTED WORKS 2000 - 2025

JASMINE MANSBRIDGE

Published by TALE MAPPER PTY LTD
Level 3, IBM Building, 1060 Hay Street
West Perth, WA 6005
Australia
www.talemapper.com

First Edition, 2025
ISBN: 978-0-6459736-5-5

Cover Design: Paul Mah - www.paulmah.com

For image credits, please refer to the index pages at the rear of the book

Disclaimer:

This collection is a work of creative expression. The poems contained within are fictional or interpretive in nature and are not intended to represent any actual persons, living or deceased, unless explicitly stated. Any resemblance to real individuals or events is purely coincidental or used with artistic license.

The views and themes expressed in these works are those of the author and do not necessarily reflect those of the publisher. The content may explore mature or challenging themes and is intended for thoughtful engagement. While every effort has been made to ensure original content, any inadvertent use of copyrighted material or similarity to other works is unintentional. Readers are encouraged to interpret the material personally, and any decisions or reactions based on these interpretations are their own responsibility.
The author world like to disclose that no Artificial Intelligence was used in the writing of this book

Cultural Warning:

Aboriginal and Torres Strait Islander readers are advised that this book contains images, names, and/or references to people who are deceased.

Acknowledgement of Country:

The author would like to acknowledge the Traditional Custodians of the lands across Australia, especially the First Nations peoples of the Katherine region in the Northern Territory, where she spent much of her formative years.
Their culture and creativity have left a lasting influence on this work.
We pay our respects to Elders past and present.

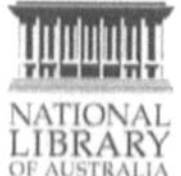

A catalogue record for this book is available from the National Library of Australia

POETRY
BURIED

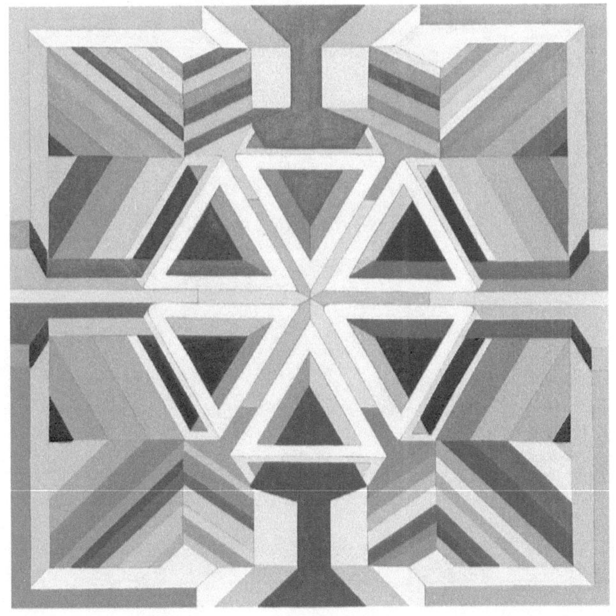

IN
GEOMETRY

To my beloved children

Caprice
Eden
Jack
Esther
Oscar

In your lifetime, may you know more love than loss

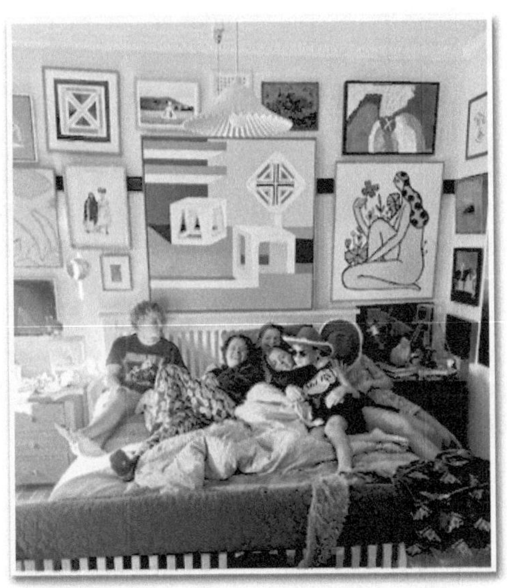

POETRY BURIED IN GEOMETRY
2000 - 2025

The exercise of gathering and compiling these poems into a book took me on an unexpected journey back through my adult life. What began simply as a project to share the 'poetry buried in geometry' aspect of my creative process had more impact on me personally than I could have anticipated.

The poems took me though some very raw, sad and hard years, each one feeling somehow healing and cathartic. They follow my highs, my epiphanies, my joys and sweet triumphs. The mysteries and the wonders of life, the world of dreams and imaginings, all these things are also explored via this lens of poetry. Revisiting my past with my current filter also came with fresh learnings and a humbling gratitude. I have done hard things and have come out the other side and I am aware there is still very likely much life to come. I am feeling brave and ready for more.

This book is a reminder, an acknowledgment and a celebration of my human experience until this point in time. I hope for you that the parts and aspects of your life that mirror mine will feel held within these pages, and that you will find your own experiences reflected in the ways they need to be, and feel comforted by the fact that you are not alone in them.

Written roughly in the years between 2000 and 2025. These words all encapsulate times in my life that were poignant for varying reasons. Unlike a real autobiography where truths are laid bear, they feel safer in their ambiguity. I feel like this level of vulnerability is therefore useful.

The focus being on the feelings without the specifics attached is a way to make the experience helpful in it's relatability. Further to this the poems are also not laid out in chronological order making them difficult to time stamp to a particular person or place.

Gifting them with a sense of anonymity.

Throughout the editing process I began to have dreams in which two horses would appear together in various scenes, one good and compliant and the other one wild and free. They made me think a lot about duality and the parts of oneself that are often in opposition to each other. I was reminded that both the light and the dark need acknowledgement and therein lies the alchemy. This is how we move forward. My book is like this in a way. All my dark and difficult times have been transmuted into appreciation and gratitude, for without those times I would not be the me now.

So while parts of the work are somewhat heavy, I have always found a way to the other side.

My losses and my grief have taught me so much about compassion and real love. They have taught me how to truly live while I am alive. My writing and my art practice have also been part of this journey. Providing a way for me to process the complexities of life. A way for me to heal and move forward. I hope you feel this via this book and that it helps you as it has helped me.

Always there is a way out and a path towards an upward conclusion. May the road rise to meet you as it has done for me over time. There are always new things around the corner. You are never as stuck as you feel. Life is truly about the accumulation of present moments. Trust that the destination is always taking care of itself.

CONTENTS

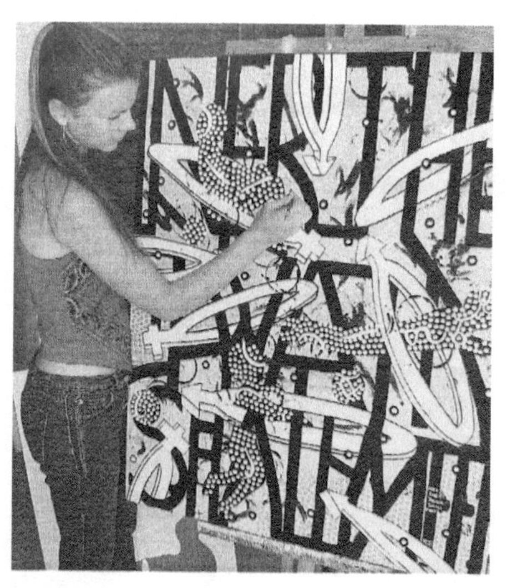

I. TIME VS EARTH

Is it ignorant to print this
Make this from trees

Words summing up
Our human earth experience

Running out of time
Running out of space

Running out of everything

But you wipe your ass
With paper freshly milled

And so why not add
To that
With something
At least somewhat literary

And kind of beautiful

Something that may remain

Beyond me and my life span

Unlike that tissue

You just flushed

2. SEEING THROUGH WALLS

Seeing through walls
Seeing through my walls

Seeing with eyes
Like globes
Neon and luminous

Casting shadows
On all I wish
To hide
All that is safe
Inside

Don't draw me out
To then fear my dark

Don't draw me out
Expecting only light

See me as I am
With an interior
Cracked and frayed

My exterior bright in contrast

To the darkness
Of my shade

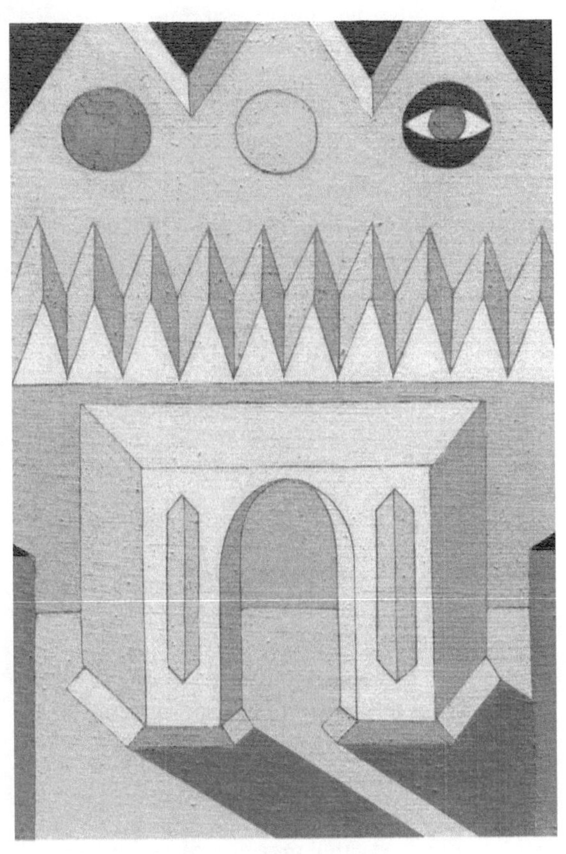

3. ALL OF THIS TIME

It's only a matter of time
Before this flame in me
Is extinguished

It's only a matter of time
Before this day
Becomes night

Before this feeling is gone
A new one arrives and this minute
Is forgotten

It's only a matter of time

I loved you so deeply once
Replaced by the tiredness
That is living and working.

It was only a matter of time

Before my eyes forgot

What you looked like the first time
What the first time felt like
What thoughts I could not dismiss

It's only a matter of time

I try and catch time and thoughts
Looking for new ways to quantify them
Looking for new ways to hold them

To hold thoughts in time
The science of this
I can't understand even though I try

To hold the present
That was us
To transcend time and space
And maybe

Distance

4. TO LOSE A BODY

To occupy only memory

Maybe that is just death

Before then before death
I want to live in every minute
In every hour

With all of this time

All time

Always

Then maybe I would then

Also never ever lose

Or have lost

You

That you and that time

Would still be

Mine

5. ONE LONG DAY

Dearest child I said

Kissing your head

Go to sleep

It has been a long day

Then I went and started my work

My art and my bread

A new day within a night

Not a even a night anymore

Life feeling like

A day in a night

Compressed time

Just one more

Long

Long

Day

(It's ok)

6. CLOSEST TO NOWHERE

Closest to nowhere
Suspended in time and place
Never lost and never found

Can't grow old
Can't leave twice

Could I change station
Could I lose you forever
Could I switch tracks
And miss you
For eternity

It's not the same I know

It's not this reality
Can't see or taste or touch

But we are here

We are still here

Closest to nowhere
Suspended in time
And place

So far from each other

Never lost however
Forever in memory and love

Intertwined
Everywhere and

Nowhere

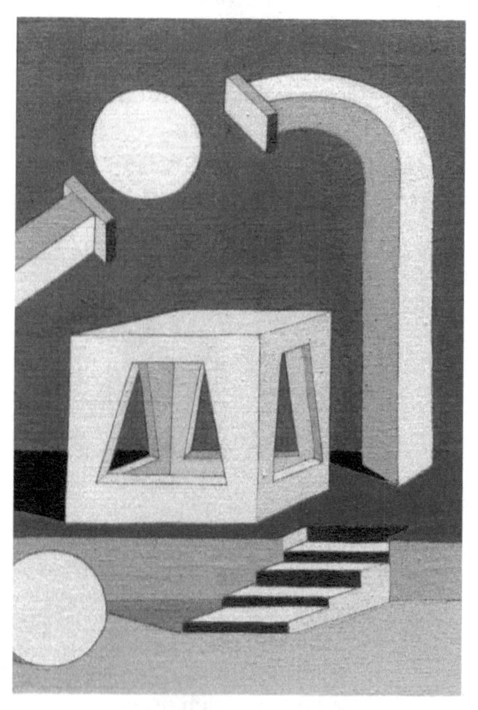

7. CATCH TIME

A stitch in time
Could have saved mine
My heart
Bound in cloth

Not one though
For prevention
Seeing stars above
Not the ground below

So I trip often
Tearing stitches
Not mending when
And as

I should

Hand me time
Time to wind back
Time to undo
Time to go slower

But I know me
Give me more and
I will want more

More stitches

More cloth

More stars

More time

More
More
More

8. HOMAGE TO TIME (JOSEF ALBERS)

I sat in front of Autumn Leaves
Where your hand worked
I sat and thought
of your thoughts

I felt them right before my own
I felt tears at the passing of time
Your art left
To do the talking

Your homage to the square
A homage to colour and form
And a homage

To time

An homage to artists

Everywhere

9. YOUR TURN FOR THE MOON

I looked at my Sun
And thought of you and the Moon
Your side of the world asleep

But then like a child
I thought of my Sun
Reflecting on the Moon

An epiphany

The Moon is mine too
The day is not separate
It is circular

It goes around

I have both the Sun
And the Moon
Even though my eye

Has lost sight of it

And you

You are still mine
As the Sun is mine
And the Moon is mine

It is just your turn

For the Moon

10. THE LIGHT BEHIND

You stand illuminated

The light behind

Setting you aglow

Streetlight

Night light

Neon light

Sunlight

Light light

I just don't want

That light

To

Go

II. THE DIVIDE OF THOUGHTS AND TIME

Your thoughts
In your space
In your time

My thoughts
In my space
In my time

Divided

So near yet so far

Can I cross your line?

Could you ask to cross mine?

We could

Share thoughts
Share space
Share time

So far and yet so very near

We share
A divide

Of thoughts and time

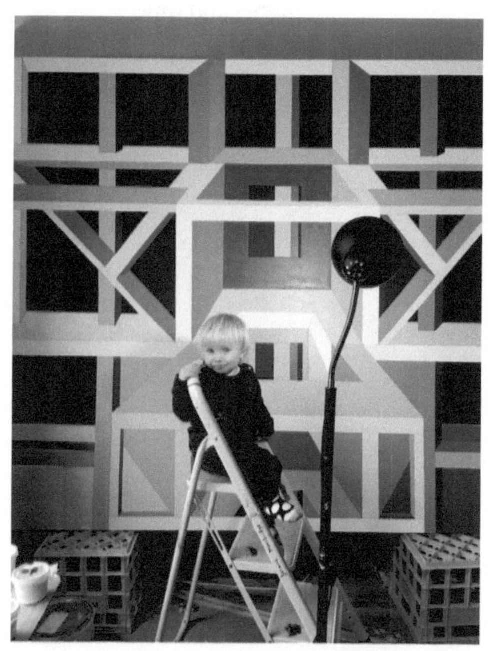

12. NIGHT BECOMES DAY BECOMES NIGHT

I am fond of that
In between space
When day becomes night
And night becomes day

That bridge between times
When the world is quiet

It is a place for painters
And writers
And crack heads and dealers

A place where

The bills are paid
The kids are asleep
The dishwasher hums

I imagine I am alone

Alone with my work

In that time
That is the time

That is nobody's time

When night becomes day

And day becomes night

13. WHEN TIME COLLIDES

On the turn of a dime

Or so they say

How fast things can change
Something happened
Time collided

With a thing
And now nothing

Will ever be the same

Again

A beginning
And an end

When fate and time

Collide

Collided

14. CLEOPATRA'S PORTAL

I painted a portal in your floor
For you to escape forever more
The tyranny of men and
Your own ambition

I wake some days
Not wanting to be me
And I wonder if you
Felt the same

Despite your position
Your glory and your fame
You oblivious to what history
Would do with your name

To give up your throne
For a babe on your breast
And so should I
I guess

Put my paintbrush
Forever down
And pick up
The washing

I should love

Best

A portal for you
And a portal for me

An escape from duty
And domesticity

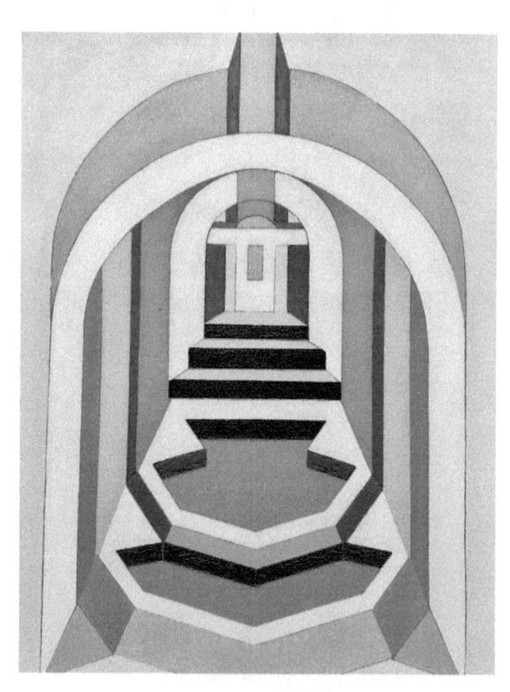

15. THE FUTURE IS BRIGHT

The future is bright
Like Cohen's crack of light

My shards and yours
My world and yours

The future is as bright

As a fluorescent
Night light

My heart and yours
My word alongside yours

We are like fools with fire
Drunk on a half-full cup

Optimism and blind love

Out of time now

And out of luck

The future is bright
With Cohen's crack of light

My shiny shards and yours
My world and yours

Through a keyhole we can see

A brighter place for you

A brighter place

For me

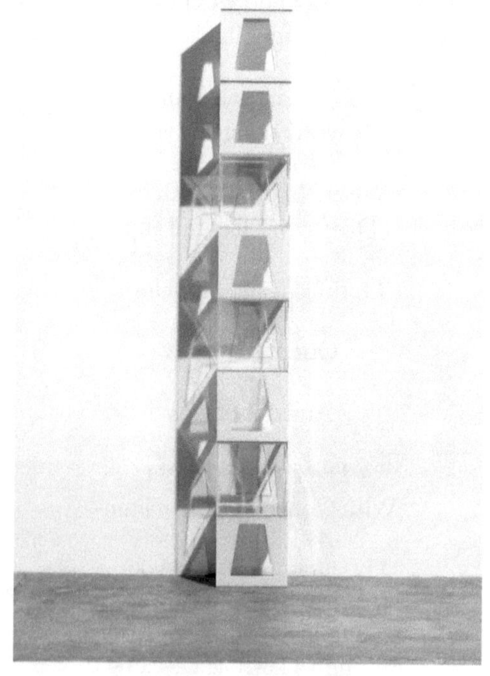

34

16. FISH AND WHALES

If you were a fish
I would throw you back
Back to depths
From whence you came

But you are not a fish

Instead a whale
Too big to ignore

A heart flooding and bursting
All-seeing and all-knowing

Too large a catch
My net too small

Yet it seems somehow
You are a perfect match

To both my lack
And my overflow

Just not what I was intending
To pull to my shore

But I guess
This is fishing

And the dredge of the ocean
Delivers you what
It sees you

Fit for

(I threw you back)

17. PAPER FEELINGS

I felt like paper that day

Like I could
Blow away

Peaceful
Letting go

Numb and blank
Like only you

Would know

Caught up in the air

Taken to anywhere

Peaceful
Letting go

Like only a freshly emptied heart

Could know

18. DRIVING WORLDS

We share this small space
One family

My eye follows a bird
Far off in a distant sky
Up
Up and then away

We talk about spelling now
You are too small for long drives

Saw s.a.w
Sore s.o.r.e
Soar s.o.a.r

We see a stone fence
You say who built that

Why
When
How

A song plays on the radio
Piano Man
And I think of long nights
Long gone

Laughter then
Loss doesn't last
We all sing silly and loud

In this small space
A microworld of our own
This present I fully absorb
Knowing that soon enough
A new journey will begin

This family
This drive
This moment will be done
This version of us will be gone

In silence then we drive on

And on

19. LET SLEEPING DOGS LIE

A sleeping dog
Is an old dog
Or a deaf dog
Or a lazy dog

My dog does not lie
It wrestles with life
Bounds endlessly
Tears on bones
And facts

Why why why

Best you say

Let sleeping dogs lie

My dog chases its tail
My dog plays the game
It never rests
It never just lies

My dog is a fool
Wise dogs
Let hard things
Like sleeping dogs

Lie

20. APEROL SPRITZ AND SMITH'S CRISPS (VENICE)

I sat in a city spilling out
With love and without
On the menu
Aperol Spritz and salty Smith's crisps

Surrounded by angels and aging walls
For which my eyes were young
But my body was old
A place of secrets adding mine
My mind in awe
Canals and portals and aging doors
All just metaphors

Then I sat at the Guggenheim
Grasping at the concept
Of passing time
Wondering at the ghosts
That hang around
And the parties
And the truths
Always true

Lives all bygone
Only art lives on

Me and Peggy entwining energy
Last century or now
Same tears and red wine vows
Venice in the summertime

The opposite of
A red dirt childhood
And outback ways
There I found a central place

Ancestral architecture
Dreams meeting daylight
Restless no more
Yet restless for more
I came home to part of me
Via Aperol Spritz and Smith's crisps

And a watery
And enveloping

City

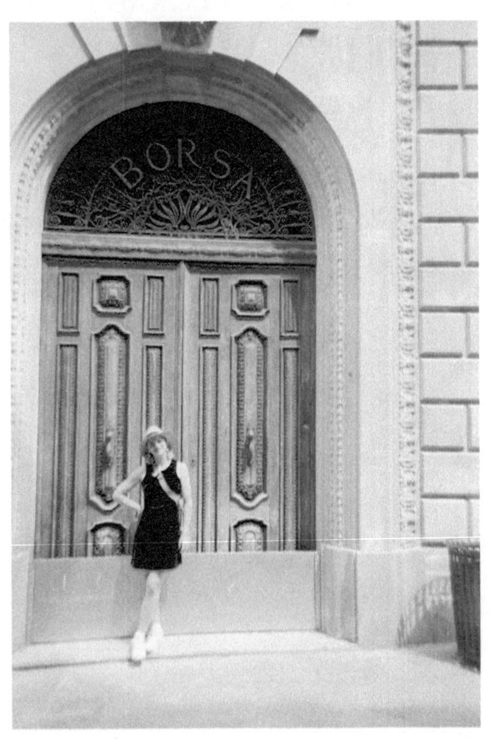
BORSA

21. SAVAGE GEOMETRY
(AFTER FRANCIS BACON)

I went and saw a Bacon show
Felt safe in the savagery
Felt him standing beside me
I too like to paint when tired you see
When the world feels soft
And the work spills out

Out of a raw place
The subconscious of night
Releasing my light
Something Bacon did

And I wanted him
To eat me that day
To be consumed
To be taken away
To be undone
To stand time still
To cry and laugh
To drink and be full
To make my own
Powerful emotional art

I went and saw a Bacon show
And it changed me

I had to leave

Of course

To raise my own sinking arm
To walk another mile
To trust my own muse

In my own time
Now this memory
This lesson
This feeling in my body
My beloved savage geometry
Buried deep inside of me

Ready to die for it
To live for it
To let it
Surge through me
This is the union

Of artist to art

22. CHECKOUT CHICK

I might just be
A checkout chick

I might just be
A checkout chick

Throw out my paints
So I can pay my bills

I might just be
A checkout chick

No longer mad

Misunderstood

I might just be

A checkout chick

Put down my paints

For good

I might

(Just not tonight)

23. RATHER DOOMED

There is an elephant in the room

It is rather cute
It is rather huge

It's the fact our world is quite doomed

If we don't wake up
It might end soon

That's not so cute
And it is huge

There is an elephant in the room

I won't say anything if you don't

And

We all can ignore

The elephant

In the room

24. MIRRORS

I have always been fascinated by mirrors. As a child, they were an entry point for wonder and something I could literally lose myself in. Time becoming warped while I looked into my own eyes to try and see what was inside of me.

To try and figure out who and what I was.

In many ways our eyes are mirrors. How we navigate the world is via the lenses and filters we place on all we see. So, if we are already the sum of our unknowns, then the ultimate mystery is what is locked inside another human being?

The entry point for higher learning then, is via another.

That it is via others we see what and who we are.

When one's own mind and soul has been searched, turned inside and out and examined. When all wonders have been pondered upon and you feel you have come to something of the end of naval gazing, yet there is still a gnawing urge for expansion, then how many more layers and infinite depths are there to be found outside of yourself? The fragments of another's interior, shown only in the glint of an eye, truly what greater marvel is there than that. When a planet can now be mapped in space and yet the human source is still impossible to trace.

We are all our own individual universe. Yet it is outside of ourselves that our inner work is revealed, where our wounds and insecurities are, where our triggers lie and where we need to grow; we learn from others. Relationships are our biggest teachers and potentially our biggest healers.

This is why they can be so profoundly hard.

Of course, there are times to be alone, to self-reflect and heal, some people for much longer than others and then there are times that those you bring close to you will help you with your own evolution, and you also with theirs.

I have seen how, in communion with another, this expansion of self can accelerate growth. It seems also that my most painful and difficult times have taught me the most. The gift of all my experiences to date has been learning how to, at the end of every day, return to the me deep inside, to my own heart centre. That I can trust myself to return to myself. This then takes the pressure off another to have to provide all your needs, which then leads to much healthier relationships with everyone in our lives.

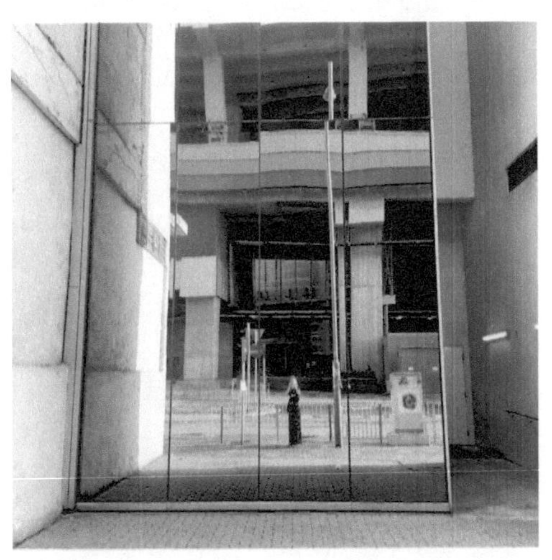

25. WHERE TO NOW

Sometimes you go through life

And you are so sure

Of everything

And then a few things change

And you

Are not sure

Of anything

You spin around

Looking for possibilities

Everywhere

You wonder how you even got

To

Anywhere

And now

Where to

From here

26. PIN THE TAIL ON THE DONKEY

I close my eyes and see my dreams
Happening as though they are today
I imagine pinning them down

My eyes shut

I know

I have to take a leap of faith

In the present
In the here
In the now

To meet the future
I am being called to

So

Sometimes you go through life
And you aren't sure of anything
But the future burns
Bright enough

To hold you and pull you
Into reality and to the present

The tough calls
You have to make

You spin around
And pin a future
To the wall

And let your eyes
Rest there and take that

Mighty
Move out of your
Comfort zone

(It will be hard, but magnificent also)

27. A PRAYER AND A MANIFESTO

For today

Help me move on
Fail fast and stay humble

For yesterday

Help me love forever
What I have loved
Forgive others fast
Forgiving also my own
Shortfalls and shortcomings

For tomorrow

Help me rise
Into the me now
To be powerful
In doing good

For ever after

Help me be kinder
Help me be wiser
Help me be stronger

Know that

If I loved you

I loved you entirely
And you were my world

If I hurt you

It caused me far more pain
Than it did you

If we moved on

It is because it was
The right thing to do
Acknowledging that

To tear down is sometimes
More meaningful
Than to continue

So tear down if you must

But then rebuild
Stand on the solid
Keep the through threads

The good that remains
Do not throw that away

But use it as the foundation
As bones for the new

For life is lived on a continuum
Nothing ever truly
Begins and ends

So take this my prayer
My manifesto of sorts

A way to be
A way to move
To love and live fully

To daily take tally
Of what truly matters

A prayer and a manifesto
My truth to the world

And to you

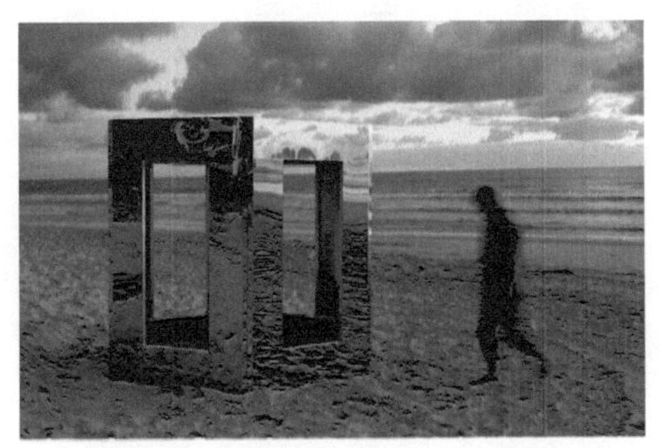

28. THE SYLVIA PLATH WAY

Oh the Sylvia Plath way
Looks attractive some days
I sit spilt cornflakes all around
Children making sound after sound
And I wonder how I got here
I feel the blood drain
From my face
From my heart
From my veins
I cannot leave
I cannot go
I cannot stay
I love you so
Your faces cherub sweet
Deserve so much more
Than a mother like me
One who paints
Even in dreams
And yet
The Sylvia Plath way
Would leave you bereft
Would leave you alone
And so I stay
In this place
In this shell
I await my return
I do not go
I do not leave
I let my veins
My face drained
The shell of me
Stay and sit and ponder
Spilt milk and chaos and cornflakes
It all washes over me and

I stay
I stay
I stay
I love you all so
So I do not go
The Sylvia Plath way
The Sylvia Plath way
I do not go
Instead I love

And I stay

(And it was more than ok)

29. GOOSEBUMPS

Not from cold
But from feeling

Feeling when you forgot
What feeling felt like
Feeling thoughts

On your body

In your head

In your stomach

Right in the pit
In the pulse and then

Goosebumps

Up your spine

Down your neck
Through your skin

And you remember

How it felt
To be alive

And full of

Feeling

Fleeting

Freeing

Feeling

Goosebumps

30. LOVERS WHO SLEEP ALONE

Eyes closed to trap feeling
Mouth open to inhale breathing
Hands closed to hold tight
Arms curled towards the night

Like a moth to a flame
Like a heart with a soul claim
Like a dance to an endless beat
Like a lost bet

You can't possibly meet

This is love inside the mind

Love both free and blind
Love you seek and then you find
Love that wells and overflows
Love that's free and no one owns

Eyes closed to trap an image

Mouth open
Breath on an ghostly photo
A memory only

Palms closed to trap endless light
Arms pulled together so tight

This is the love of the lovers
Who sleep alone at night
The love only you own
The love of the light
The truest love of your life

You are the love of your life

Your own breath
Your first and your last
This is love

Inside the mind
The truest love is your own

The lover who sleeps
Alone

31. CRUMBS

Why is it

That in love

I have settled for

The crumbs from your table

So

Much

Food

Lying

All over

Other people's floors

And yet here I am

Starving

Hungry

For more

No

More

32. FOLDING

At my starting point
I was a cool crisp
Calm quiet flat sheet

Of paper

I let myself be folded
To fit the first time

And then another time
Folded another way

Another crease
Another line
Folded again
Time after time

Folded ideas
Folded form
Folded ways

And then into the
Smallest of shapes

I had finally become

A tiny small square
A fragment of myself

A shape which could
Fit anywhere
And please
Anyone
Anytime

That time is no more
The folding no more
The folding all done

Back at my starting point
I was a cool crisp
Calm quiet flat sheet
Of paper

As I am again

33. FEEDING DREAMS

Feeding dreams
Is the only way
I can be me
Leaving the present

Adding fuel to

Future fires
Future places
Future desires
Future versions

Of me
Yet to be

Feeding dreams

Closing eyes
Going to places
Deep inside

Where all is hidden

All is mine

Sometimes the past
And the present
Best be
Left behind

Best to feed

The dreams waiting

For all is beautiful
In a future

Life

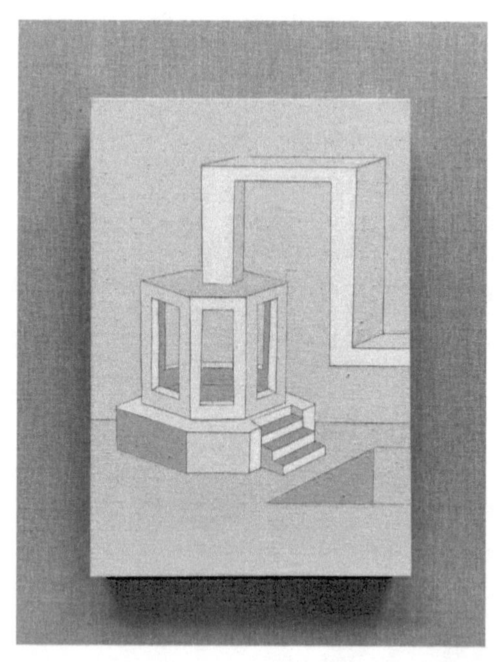

34. THE GIVE AND TAKE OF TIME

The give and take of time
In these bodies
Yours and mine

Time gave me you and you

And you and you and you

Gave me my babies
Gave me love true
Gave me

Me

Me more fully

And as each
Sun rises and falls
Time takes some

Takes one

Will take all

The give and take of time

Time gave me parents
Then time made me one

Time gave me
Everything

In equal measure

Time
Time

The give and take

Of time

35. SLEEP OF THE GODS

My dear

Sleep the sleep of the gods
Like one who has fought well
And won

Like one who wears a lion
On thy chest
Like one who has known love
Yet knows how still
To love afresh

My dear
Sleep the sleep of the gods
Like one who has rolled the dice
And won

Like one who wears gold in his ears
Like one who knows the words
But new words still appear
For you to hear

My dear

Sleep the sleep of the gods
No salt water for your tongue

No shadows block
Your sun

No violin for your tears
No anguish left
In your dreams

My dear

Sleep the sleep of the victor
One who has walked
The earth right

Sleep with the 1000 loves
Who loved you by your side
Sleep my dear

Sleep well

36. TWO NIGHTS IN VENICE

A thunderstorm
A delayed plane
Venice via Verona
In floods I came

I wandered lost
Till the sun came up
In dark canals
Following my wanderlust
Fatigue superseded
By travel dreams

The canals
The bridges

The facades

Déjà vu at every turn

I was in the city
Of my minds eye
Of my drawing pen
Of my sleep time wanderings

So familiar yet so foreign

Two nights
Not long enough
Yet better than
No nights at all

What fresh eyes see
I can't explain
Worth more though
Than 100

Average days

37. TEMPORARY

Would you let me
Set my tent up here

I lost my way you see

Somewhere between

Point A and point B

They said it was
An easy track

But I skipped some steps
And I can't go back

Or forward

So here I am
Stuck you see

Somewhere

Between

Point A and point B

Everything
Feeling

So very
Very

Temporary

38. THE DREAMERS AND I

My friend the dreamer said
One day in steel birds
In the sky we will fly

My friend the dreamer said
There are aliens close by
One day they might

Stop in and say hi

My friend the dreamer said
We are connected
Your soul and mine

One day science will explain

The how of this
And the when
And the why

One day

Everything

Unknown

Will be known

Even the mystery

Of all the dreamers

And I

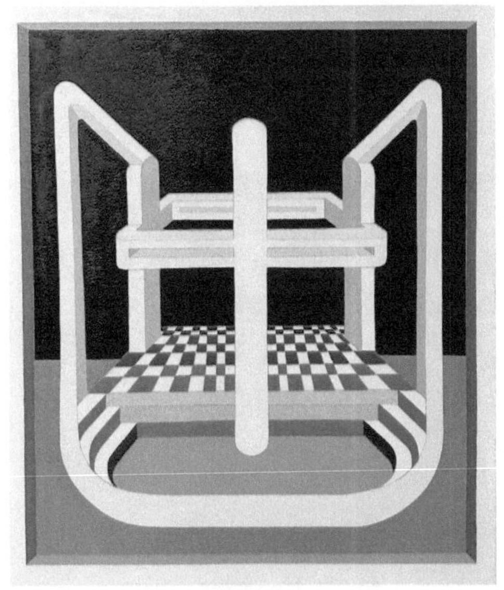

39. SOLITUDE

What of this solitude
Of the unsettling of it
Then the settling
Back into it

Of days
Rising and falling
Old rhythms
Slipping away

No new poetry
No new refrains

What of this solitude
Thoughts and walls
Walls and thoughts
Memories leave
And memories haunt

And the future seems

So far away

When it creeps along
Quiet day by quiet day

What of this solitude
Is this all
That remains
Yet slowly
All falls away

Letting the stillness settle
Into my bones

Waiting for new poetry
New refrains

This season of winter and rest
Till spring returns
Till life returns

Again

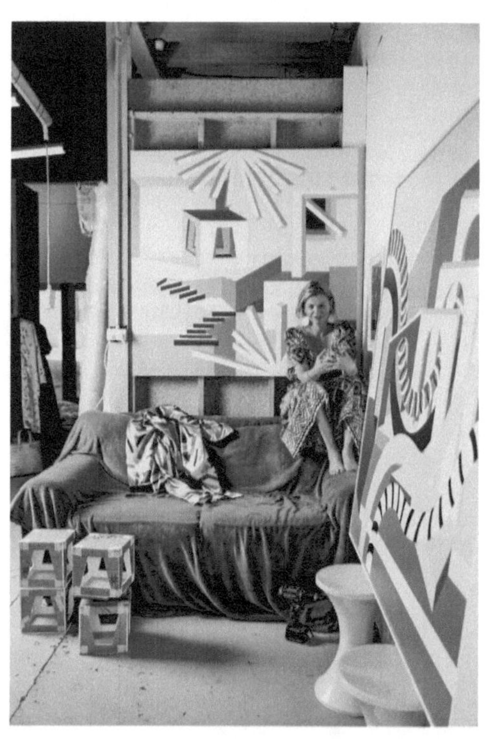

40. NEW LIFE CALLS

Trees far off call
Seas call and creeks call

Life calls and says

Come back
Come back

To yourself

Like ground fallow in winter
Like the pruning of dead wood

There is a burst of green life
That awaits

But first

It is a cut and it is a end
It is a fire

Humbled
Returned
To your truths

Returned to your roots

Come back
Come back
To yourself

To your own

Inner lands and inner seas
Inner creeks
There there is
A burst of new life

That awaits

Awaits you
And me

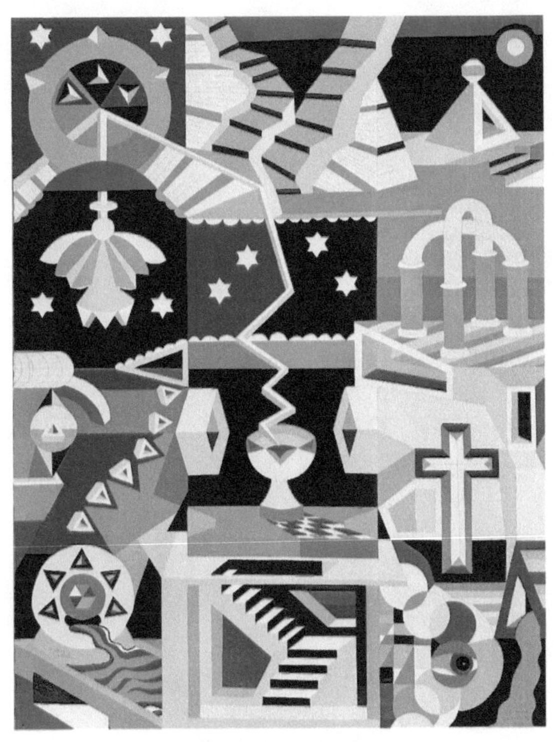

41. WHAT SITS IN SPACE

Always impossible
The distance always

Too much

The risk of loss
Always too great

The beauty of it all

The aesthetics
The romance
The expansiveness

Of love and longing

Too much to take

We learn to sit
We learn to accept

The worlds between us

Albeit the waste

We learn to sit

To sit in this space

42. MOON LADY

I lay on grass
In damp and dark
And felt the Moon
Looking down on me

Embraced by her warmth
On this dark night
Her familiar face
Reminding me

Of my infinity

The awareness that
Her eternal glow
Reflected on those
Long before my own

The cells of her
A part of me
A part of them
Of our collective

Energy

And so

On this green I lay
My back growing damp
My heart softening

Perhaps softer than

It has ever been

Moonlight
Moon bath

78

Moon lady
Moon heart

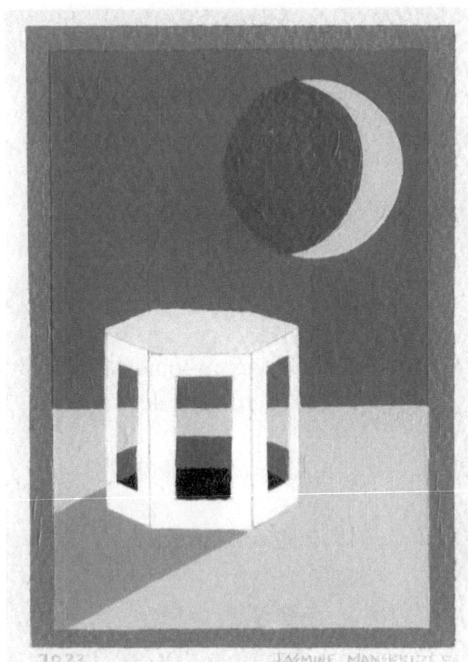

43. FLY

Do you recall
When I only crawled
Afraid my dear
Of the fall

And you said

Fly

Fly

Fly

I am lifting my wings
I am getting close

Closer to the sky

To all you foretold

Learning to fly

Fly

Fly

Fly

44. RIVER OF TEARS

A river of tears let go
A wall no one could hold
You said goodbye
And my breath left

I felt my hands and my feet

Go cold

You were
Too much for the world
For yourself
For me
Too brittle
Too soft
Too tender

Too lost

So my breath left
For a minute
It followed you

And then
And then

I felt my hands and my feet

Go from cold
To warm

I am also so soft
Too soft
To stay
Yet too soft

To leave

I can not go too
I have to stay
For this world

Still needed me
Still needs

Me

Especially as it lost

You

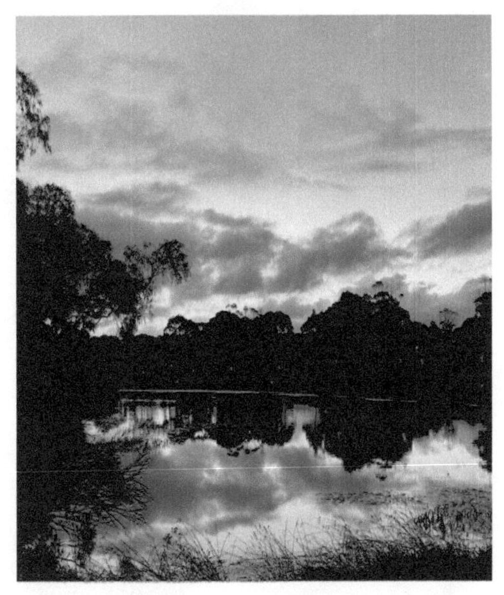

45. WATCHING FOR THE WIND

It wasn't until the sky disappeared

My wings disappointed and weary
By my side sitting quietly

Resting now
Still now

Blood beginning to flow again
To the tips and back again

New feathers forming
Waxed and shining
While I sat and waited

Watching for the wind
Waiting for the currents
For the sky to open again

To take me back
To where I could soar

Once more

Yet

While my body and soul rested
Gaining strength
In the stillness
In the expansion inside

It wasn't till the sky fell that I realised

That strong wings emerge not
While you are flying
But while you are planted firmly

On the ground

46. LAST THINGS

Thinking about last things
Sinking into the bittersweet melancholy

Of this

The irony of last things
Being that
At the time you do not know
They are last things

Last dance
Last word
Last joke
Last dinner
Last birthday
Last Christmas

Last things

And now I reflect on this
Woken by it in the night
By the very thought

This very human dread
Of last things

Resisting letting go
Of last things

Of you

The last of us
The last of me
The last of you

Till our next eternity

Last things

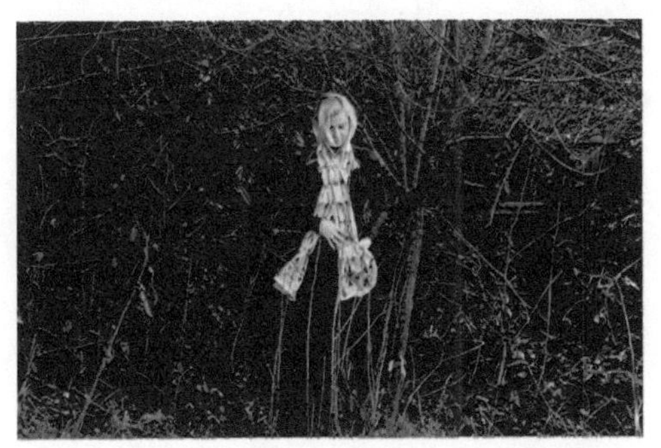

47. HEART SHAPED WOMB

I feel a melancholy now
That time has passed
And I let it slip away

Wishing myself
Here or there
Everywhere

But in that present
Where you were

Rising above
Those baby years
With their weary joys
And endearing tears

So many things asked of me

The selflessness
The tiredness

But yet here I am now
Taking stock of all
I have taken for granted

My heart expanded
Etched and blessed

Arms forever imprinted

Breasts and body
Remembering

Nothing erased
Nothing lost
Forever held

My heart shaped womb
My muscle memory
Embedded with the feeling of you

In my arms
And in my

Heart shaped womb

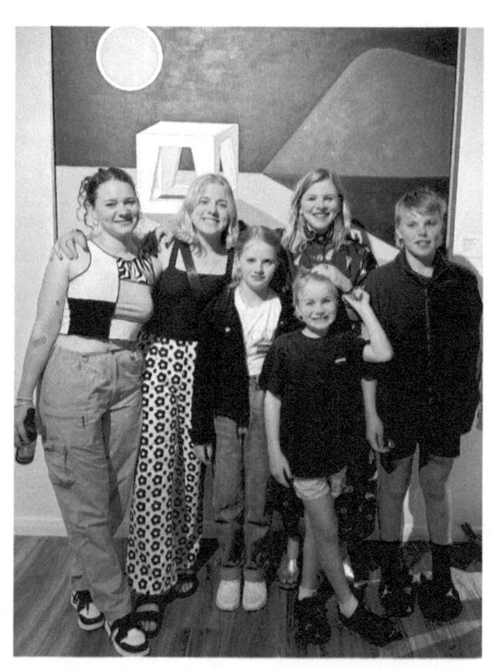

48. FULL FORCE

When I let myself love again
Do let it be like this

Full force

Like one who may die
On the morrow

Like one

Who has

Never loved
Never lost

Like a fresh flower
Like a fruit ripe

Innocent
Not jaded
Not ashamed

Exuberant

Unafraid

To love with

Full force

49. LAND ON YOUR FEET AGAIN

What is life

But falling and rising
And twisting and turning

If you are lucky

You will rise
More than you fall

You will turn
More than you twist

You will land
With your two feet

On the ground

If you are lucky

If you live
If you learn
If you adapt
If you change

Then you can rise

Fall

Twist

Turn

Land on your feet again

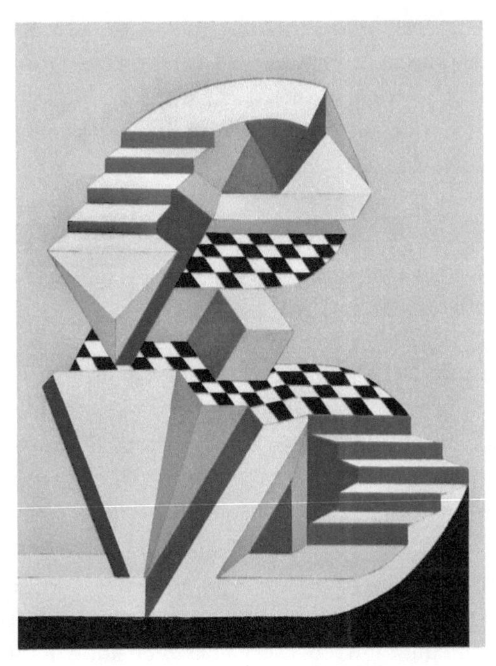

50. CURIOSITY

If I am safe within myself, then curiosity is the natural extension of that.

So how can I not be endlessly curious? The questions I have today, I will have answers for tomorrow, and my words today will have lost their weight as a new idea gives way to a new thought and a new line of enquiry.

This is the ever-expanding nature of curiosity. Curiosity is a way to transcend hurt and access compassion. For if you are curious about the other, then you can view situations as an outsider. Curiosity is a way to ensure you bounce back more quickly from disappointment and is a path towards greater resilience.

You can never ask too many questions. Someone who values you will be happy to answer them. Anyone who feels they need to withhold things from you does not deserve you or your curiosity.

In addition, wounds today will heal and be but a distant memory if they are viewed with the sense of self-compassion. I want my life to be always expanding and for me to be increasingly comfortable out of my comfort zone. As I see it, if I am present in my curiosity, then I will always be following my truest path.

So this is where I stand, writing this, willing to look outside of my own impermanent state of thinking. To not be completely fixed in my viewpoints. Looking for mirrors everywhere. To know I am not just my mind, so to remain curious about my thought patterns. To cultivate self-awareness via that. To be always asking, weighing up, and returning to the next best thing.

To be brave enough to always ask the questions that may not have the answers I want to hear and to unravel the emotions around that. Why am I afraid of this sometimes, and why is it that another person's opinions not matching mine can feel troublesome? I am aware that I need to deal with the sense of separation that can arise when this occurs. To return to me when there is a gap, and be okay with that.

To not put my illusions and projections over another's reality, and accept truths as they are revealed to me. To learn about me via others. To learn about others via me.

To let curiosity be the conduit for growth.

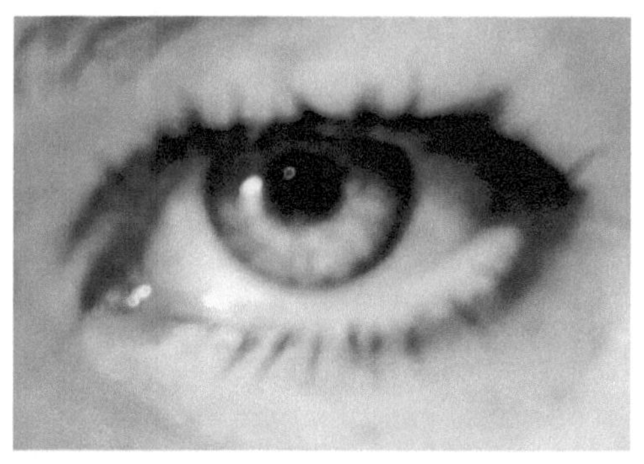

51. FOOLISH AND FROZEN

Here we are
As foolish and as frozen
As animals in front of headlights at night
And I wonder of the route we came
The many roads to here

I wonder of the fate of us

Two people
Many paths

And then a junction
And why it is so hard
To walk away
Before anything is broken

But when everything is broken

If this ship could sail
Would it whisk away
Or would it dash on rocks
Sinking then
Disappearing into the sea
Would we ride waves
Together so much stronger
Like the great loves of old
Who conquered all

Could this be you and me

However

We freeze not sail

We let it be and let it go
History says we were
Immobile
Foolishness or bravery
No one knows

We let it be
Let it go
We lay anchor
Abandon ship

Travel separate roads

52. THIS HORSE I RIDE

So you know my mind
And the valleys and mountains

On a raging horse
I sometimes ride

To arrive

Again

At the same destination

Self-acceptance

Quiet

Resignation

Nostrils no longer flared

Resting on the flat lands

Until she's

Called

To ride

Again

So you know my mind
And the valleys and mountains

On a raging horse

I sometimes ride

53. DANCING STARS

Just before the skies fall
And the sea crashes foreshores
Before the world moves
And the oceans lose

Their gravity

Let my lonely cells
Meet the star dust
Their family as such
And clusters of friends

The magnetic
Bursts of matter
Thrown together
By chaos

Making order

Before the forests are felled
And the rivers swell
And the planets whirl
And the dirt rains

And the land spills

Let my blood run
My humanity split
From this one body
And become
Something more

My soft being torn
For all to see
The joy and pain
Of my vulnerability
Hid now inside of me

Let me be one
With the Moon and the Sun
The planets and
The dancing stars

Let the world see
The living fibre of you
The fibre of me
In this bloody fight

We call humanity
Let its clawing scraping joy
Be ripped and drawn

Right out of me

Let my gold be seen
And my gemstones be touched
Let my flesh be felt

And a calm wash over
My large and wild

And weary

Beating
Human

Heart

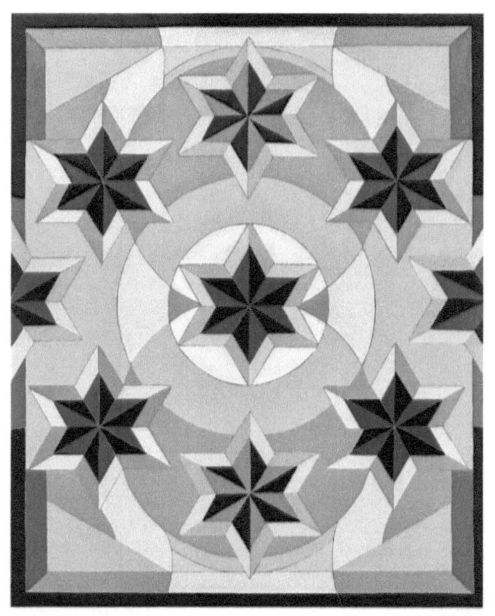

54. BOTTLES UNBROKEN

The sea lapping at my feet
This body of water
Touching all the world
An affection of sorts
A gathering of minds
And thoughts

Bottles not broken
But whole
Carrying messages
With vibration
Across these unseen shores
To this wee wave

All of this endless
Yet contained
Beauty of living
Held in this luminous blue sea

So I stand grateful
For the gift of life
For the power in me
Connected by and to all
And everything

I was asleep
But now I have awoken

The sea lapping at my feet
This body of water
The circle unbroken

The water connecting all and me

For now and infinity

55. GHOSTS AND DREAMS

Dreams I'd pinned with paperclips
Around the edges of my mind
Dreams I sent into the air
With balloons I sent them high

Then I dreamt I was a ghost
A ghost just chasing dreams
Shadows I was chasing
Beyond the valley of the seen

A ghost dreaming paperclip dreams

So I pulled out all the things I'd kept
Then slowly let them go
The ones up in the air
I set them all afloat

In my dreams adrift
I set my dreams afloat

Then with tears I kissed the ghost
I pulled her right through me
Her shadow disappeared
Then both of us were free

To be empty is also to be free

Salty tears ran down my face
And I felt my feet sink down
My heart swelled in that place
My feet flat on the ground

No dreams now just quiet me
I lay then on the earth
And looked up at the sky

To be empty is also to be free

Kissing clouds and remembering
All the dreams and ghosts gone by
Dreams only pinned with paperclips

Around the edges of my mind

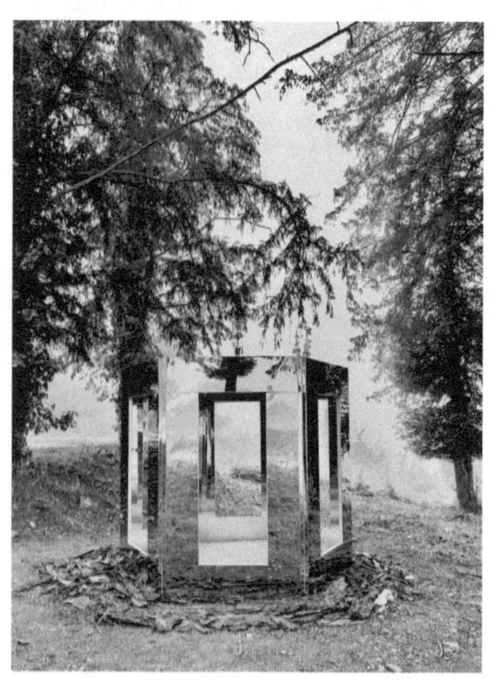

56. GAME OF DUST

I have been digging deep
Deep into earth
I thought I had
Already mined dry
My words spent
My wings weary
Every bit rung out

Now truth and night are nigh

Nothing left but paper skin
All washed out
Red and thin
Seeping to the ground
Skinless I have felt
As I sink into the earth
Taking stock of things

Never lost and never found

Remembering it's a game of dust we play

And only love remains
Yes only love remains

And for my warm warm heart
The cost of this heated blood

Has been so very high

And yet I would give everything
Rather than let it while alive
Slowly sadly weakly die
For my heart and for love

I will ring all out and drip-dry

Every very last feeling
Plunge it into darkness
Pull back a bloodied curtain
Still my anxious heart
Cease my tears from falling

And rise
Rise
Rise

Play this game of dust

With love

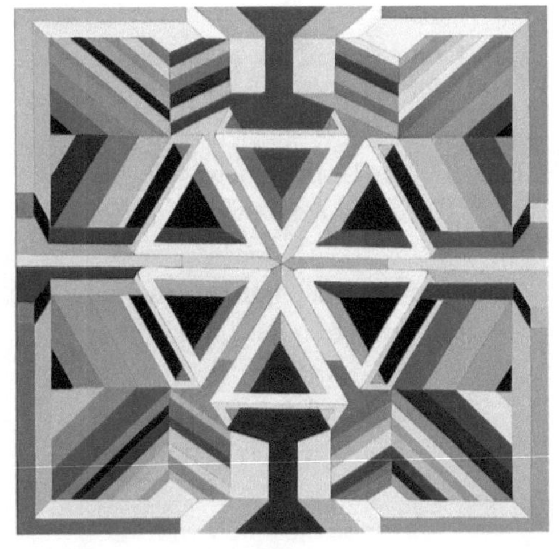

57. YOU BE THE WOLF

You be the lonely wolf
And I will be the stream
You can sit by me

Lick your wounds clean

Come lie with me at midnight
Howl at the heavy Moon

You be the lonely wolf
And I will be the stream

You can weep into my waters
And drink to quench your thirst

I am cool and deep and endless
I rise from the belly of the earth

You be the lonely wolf
And I will be the stream

Together we can heal our wounds

And we can dream

A brand-new dream

58. CLEOPATRA AND ANTONY

There is a way to the Moon
Said Cleopatra to Antony

Ahh no ... he said
That's just a fantasy

She bit his cheek
And kissed him playfully
She said we don't know
What is real or what is fantasy
But one day the future
Will make gods of you and me

Gods of you and me

Who knows what's real
What the future will make
Of you and me

Gods we could be

The earth is round she said
As she turned over in her bed

Ahh no... he said
That's just fantasy

She kissed his feet
And stood to leave
She said we don't know
What is real or what is fantasy
But one day the future
Will make gods of you and me

Gods of you and me

Who knows what's real
What the future will make
Of you
And me

Gods we could be
Eventually

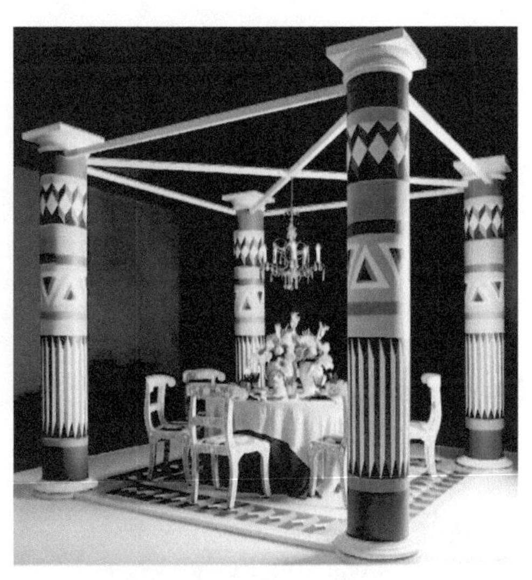

59. WALK ME HOME

Rest rest rest

All we need is second best
There's steam enough
To reach the finish line

We're allowed to take our time

Be be be

Come and sit alone with me
Backs to paperbark trees
Like sky and water we are free

Marrow growing in our bones
Moss gathering on our stones

We walk each other home
We walk each other home

Be be be

Come and sit alone with me
I will walk you home
You will never be alone

Alone

Rest rest rest

Your head now upon my chest

You walk with me alone

We walk each other home

60. LOVE MAKING LIFE LIVE ON

An expanse of light and love opened
Asking her to close her eyes
And fall into a luminous
White and blue sky

Into an unknown promised land
Every lost love there
Waiting

Imagine that
It all being returned

And then all her souls
Weightless joy
Came flooding forth to catch her
Circling curling hands around her

Timeless
Transcendant
Not human

Seeping through her skin like water
To the roots of a unseen tree
Some love is like that

Watering the heart always
And for eternity

Traveling with you from plane to plane
From one dimension and back again
Love making life
Live on and on and on
And in you

For those who see

The valley is always open
There is always a crack
In the luminous

White and blue sky

61. WORTHY WEARINESS

And here I lie
A kind of early yet old maiden
A body given to babes
A breast to the earth

Sinking into this bed
Days full and back again

Hands full
Head full

And if 'twas not
For the divine love in my heart

Still longer days they'd be
Alone in bed I'd be

Instead of dreams of thee
To keep me company

So I rest my weary head
Shut my tired eye
Enfold myself to myself

And sigh a good night sigh
Grateful for an ever full life

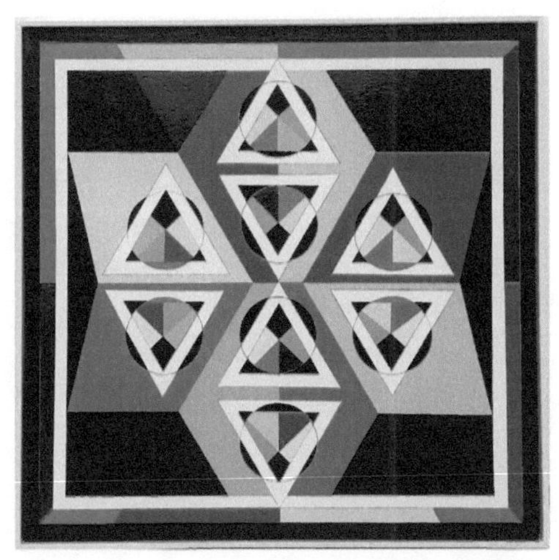

62. WORTHY OF A DREAM

I have felt invisible
Unseen as though a ghost

And so to make my work
Is to bring my body home
And me into this

Mortal world

So they can say one day

She existed

She did

She had thoughts and ideas

She was worthy of a dream

I feel visible and I feel seen
I have my work

To bring me into this

Mortal world

I am worthy

Of

A dream

63. THE ROOTS OF POTTED PLANTS

Like a potted plant I seek the Sun
Move with it from room to room
Yet I wonder about the garden outside
Where things grow and do not move

Sometimes I wish I were like that too
Satisfied and able to withstand
The Sun the wind and the rain
To sit all in one place and never feel
A growing pang

Yet I outgrow my pot
I need new soil
New air
New light
I do

My roots get restless
Twine around themselves
Leaching every good thing
Needing more and more
New pots and new soil
New air and new Sun

This is me

Here I am waiting for a new home
A new pot and a new place
Waiting to start the process of growing
All over again

Perhaps one day I will find perfection
A garden where like an oak
I will be planted

Where my roots will never reach an end
Where my heart will find its forever soil
And where the eternal Sun

Will shine forever more

64. OARS AND BONES

We sucked the marrow
From each other's bones
I wasted wanted and spent you
And you hid from me

The river between us
Grew wide and deep

Narrowed eyes
Never able to see
Your shore or mine
Hearts becoming invisible
Hidden in our fogs

Alone

And nothing now left
Could wade us through
The water's murky and deep

And so we moved on
Each gathered what was left
Looked for the good
Said goodbye with tenderness

Tenderness
Too little too late

Set oars to boats and onwards
Onwards on waters afloat
Grew marrow back into our bones
Carved new oars for those new boats

Forever more
What floats floats
What sinks sinks

Our bones are what we cannot leave
We put them in rivers and in seas
Fleshed with tears and humility
Love and shared humanity

Oars and bones

Lessons of skin
Lessons of blood and kin
Lessons of letting go

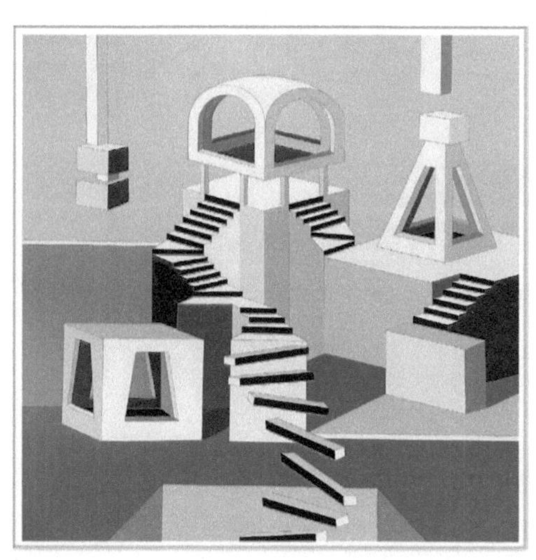

65. DON'T START A FIRE TO PUT IT OUT

What are we to each other
What are these feelings we feel

Do we stoke this fire
Or douse it with water now

Is it just an illusion
That when I see your skin
I want to be in it
To slide under

To see and touch your heart
Is this just the beginning
Or is this an end

It's beginnings
I am most afraid of
Ends I have mastered
Ends I can quantify

Ends I can make sense of

But this space I am finding
So quietly hard

Because beginnings are messy
They traipse through the unknown
Through voids and valleys
Chemical love mixed with hope

So what are we if we ignore this
Squash the connection

Will it disappear
Will it dissipate

Or will we have subverted
And twisted fate

For my fear is that to touch you
Is to want you
And then to want you
Is to risk losing you

Yet it is also to touch life
To potentially bring air
Back into me
And back to you

To start a fire
We won't need to put out
To desire more and have more
That it won't consume us
But rather burn back
What does not belong

To melt us into
Gold and silver
Every fine metal
An alchemy of being

We could lose ourselves
In ourselves forever

Lost somewhere in our skins
And deep in our hearts

It would not matter then
For in the losing
We will have found everything

We will have started a fire

We need never have

To put out

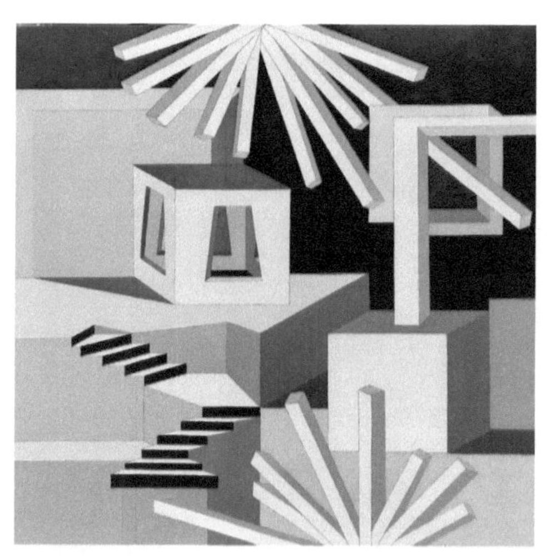

66. LEFT BUT NOT LEAVING

In a dream you called to me
Beckoned to me
To come beyond the veil
But I stood at that threshold
One I could not cross

My will and body strained
My ears burning to hear
My heart big and wide like an ocean
A river I could not traverse
Or cross

And in a dream you spoke to me
Words I could not understand
Could not know what it was
What you could want
From me

And all the day you followed me
Like a cloud upon my sky
Ever present yet still so far away
And I wonder of this I do
I wonder what is me and what is you

What should I do
How can I know
Where is it your heart is wanting to go
What do you want and need from me
A mere ghost and a memory
Set apart yet not set apart

From me

Forever close
Forever far
Left but not leaving
Not ever gone
Not ever done

Left but not leaving

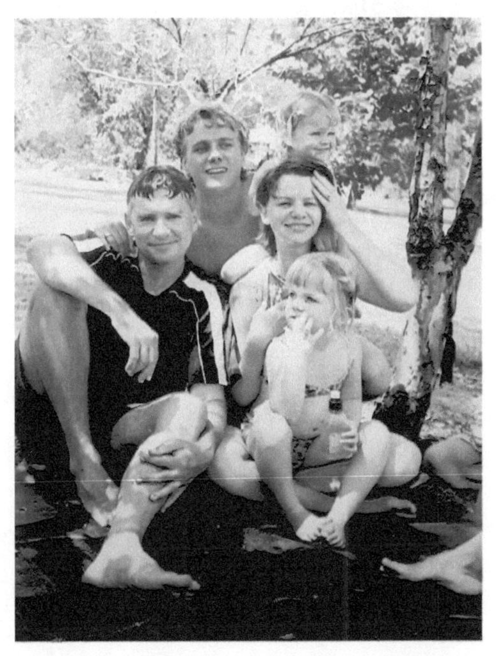

67. EYES TO THE SKIES

Eyes to the sky always
And how ye trip and fall
The folly of the ground
You miss

And yet
The glorious things you see
The rainbows and sunsets
And clouds their melancholy

You may fall
But you will higher rise
With your eyes fixed on
The heavenly skies

All above
Ner below lies

Eyes to the skies

Eyes to the skies

68. HEALING

I have always sought to move forward whilst acknowledging that the past lives on in present parts of ourselves. Sending ripples into the waters of today, which need reconciling, so that those ripples don't become waves that can overturn and eventually sink us. Developing self-awareness around wounds means we don't so easily recreate toxic situations or repeat past mistakes. Healing is seeing.

It is important to work towards tending to and alchemising all the parts of oneself and to integrate new learnings and to recalibrate regularly as we go. This is the goal, albeit it sometimes you feel you are not progressing and like it is forever two steps forward and one step back.

Honestly, though, while you are doing the work, at the same time, I think it is so important to celebrate your highs and lows and to not compare your journey with anybody else.

You have to also live. To be able to also hold space for joy and self-appreciation. To be present and not always looking back. Sometimes that is the healing. To realise you are no longer obsessed with the past. Our wounds are as individual as our healing process; therefore, it is important to love all the versions of oneself and not just the one that others would celebrate. To love the part of us in progress as well. To love our damaged parts.

There are never right or wrong answers as to how to do anything really, there are just better ways and less helpful ways. Ways that serve you more than others and ways that take you off your path and take more time to reroute.

Go easy on yourself when you feel you have taken a step in the wrong direction, as it will just be a fresh reminder of where you need to take extra care. Contrast is a powerful tool for learning and remembering what you do and do not want to experience in your life. It illuminates where you may need to build some more self-awareness and perhaps source some outside support.

Every day is a new opportunity to change and reroute. Healing and growth requires patience and a willingness to better understand yourself and to look honestly at your patterns. This is where other people, the mirrors in your life and curiosity about who you are and how you got to here play a key role.

I am grateful to be where I am as a person these days. When I see rainbows in the sky, I am reminded that every moment holds the opportunity for a new beginning. Every day is a brand-new day and the first day of the rest of your life.

You've got this.

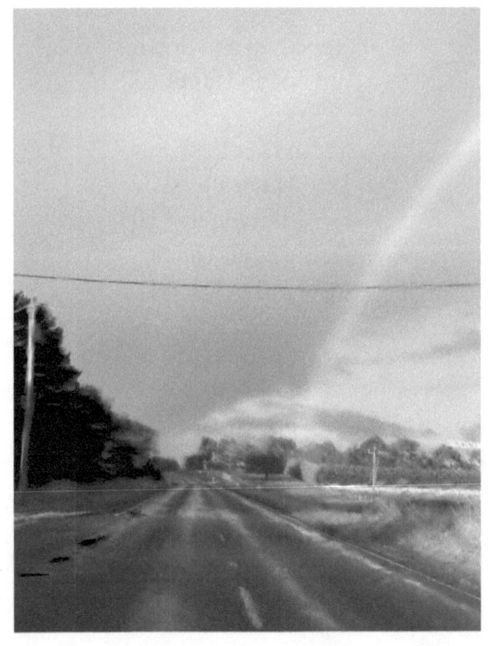

69. REBORN

Tipped up and down
And out and emptied

And yet Love
Magically
Like water
Returns and finds
A brand-new level

A new skin
To be filled
Is formed

We all survive
And then we thrive

Miraculously

We are reborn

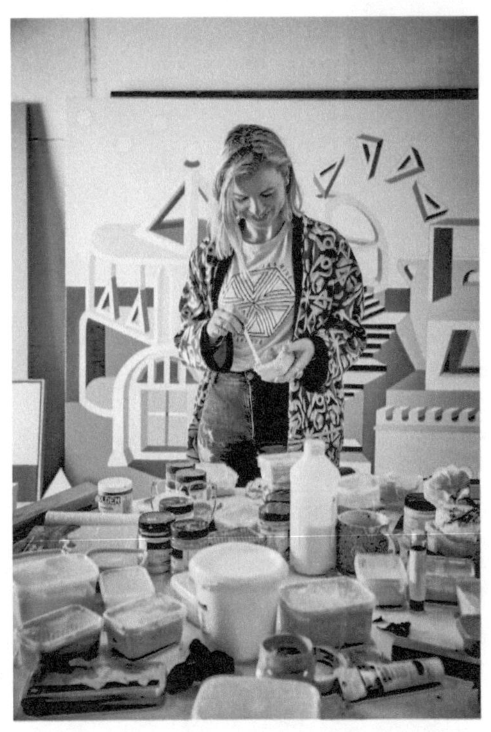

70. IF YOUR HUSBAND DIES

If your husband dies
People bake you biscuits
Leave casseroles and bread
At your front door
Mysteriously someone
Mows your lawn

But

If you get a divorce
You get radio silence
Supermarket stares

Did she have an affair

And if a husband still lives
But does not live
With you anymore
Be prepared to be ignored

Put your own bins out

And

Hold your tongue
Be gracious
Be expansive
Be resilient
Do what is best for the children
Put up with societal bullshit

Smile though tears

Now and now and forever more

So

Be kind to the women
Who are widows
With living

Ex -husbands

(Be kind)

71. THE BODY AS A COMET

I imagine myself to be
Both body and shadow
A comet made of cells
Shooting blindly

Trusting that the space
In front of me
Continues to clear

That infinity has no brick wall
That it forever holds me dear

For in the nothingness
I feel held
Like I can't bump into
Or break anything

Can't be hurt or hurt
Can't bleed

For hearts need gravity
Need to be still
To feel

Need to be cut to weep
Faster than
The speed of light

I pour out and out
And out

I fly faster than all

Faster than

A body
A shadow
A cluster of
Cells

Skin
Dark
Done

I am

A comet made of seeds
Shooting blindly

Always forward
Always

On

Always
Seeking

Heat
Light
Sun

Soil I can
Plant myself in
Earth

And you

I shoot on
And on
No fear here
Waiting for my landing

My place
My destination

To appear

(Calling all the beautiful and good things to me always)

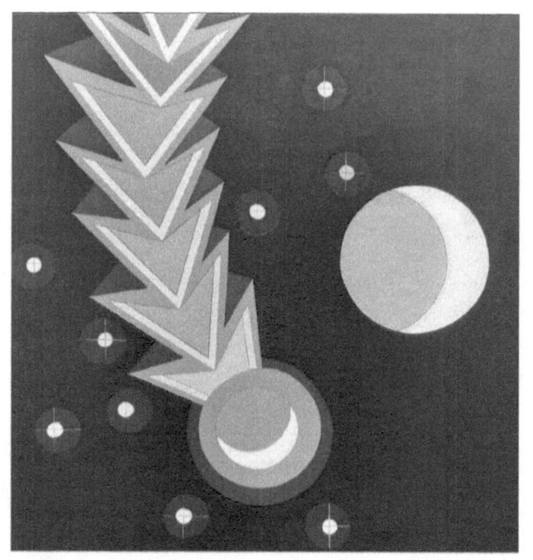

72. GRANDMOTHER OF MY DREAMS

There is a grandmother I visit in my dreams
She has always been there
A reoccurring theme

And tonight I went to see her but her house was quiet
She had left me a note to say she had died
And I woke up crying
The grief so very real

As I realized that this grandmother
Was not my grandmother at all
Yet I loved her and had seen her in my dreams so often
And then I thought of who
Could I tell if I didn't have her
To tell

Of my loss and my grief
And how alone I was now
And then I cried to think
I could lose you too

That like her you also might disappear
Into the ether beyond
This precious dream person
Whom I really knew not
This precious dream person
Who the whole world forgot
But not me
I loved and I remembered

But no more visits now she was gone
Even dream worlds can come to an end
I cried then again my heart so very full
And so very on edge
So open and so vulnerable

As I remember myself standing at her closed door
Saying goodbye in an alternate quiet

Surreal and subconscious world

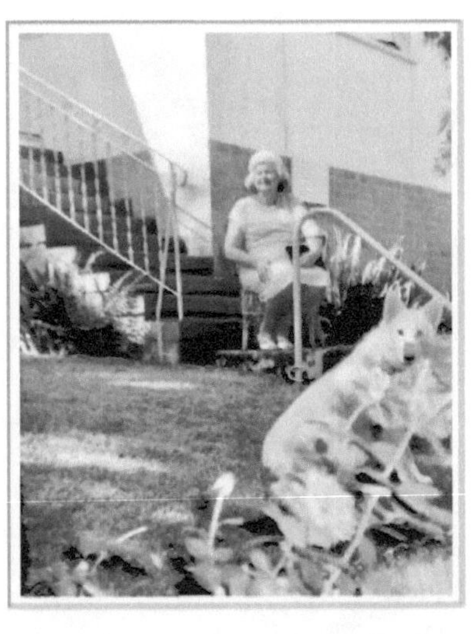 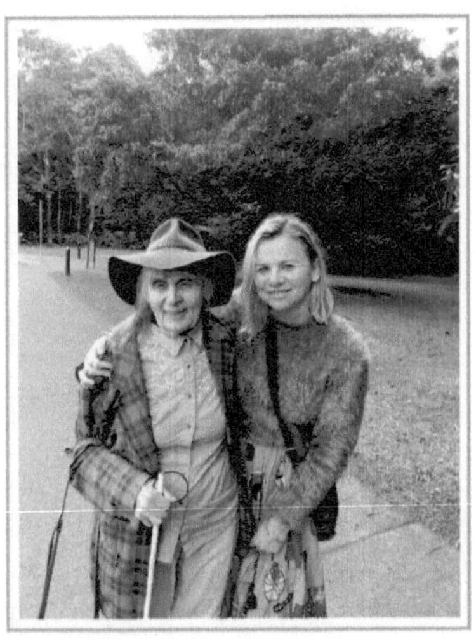

73. HEART VINE

I am trying to unwind
My little heart vine
From seeking the Sun
Atop your tall tree

Seeking your light
And your vibrancy

This little vine
Took on a new form

And is finding it hard
To go back
To the place

Hence from
Whence it
Came from

So

Back to flat lands
Back to shade
Back to the quiet of
Mine own

Heart space

74. I HAVE PUT MY DRAGON TO SLEEP

I have put the dragon to sleep
I have put the dragon to sleep

Kissed her head

Whispered rest for awhile
Suck in your fire
Your heat
Let it warm you now

I have put the dragon to sleep
I have put the dragon to sleep

She lies deep inside of me
She lies peacefully

Quietly
She waits
For her time

I have put the dragon to sleep
I have put the dragon to sleep

She awaits for a future place
When love will resurrect
What's dormant
Will rise again

I have put the dragon to sleep
I have put the dragon to sleep

Maybe it will sleep a week
Maybe a year
Maybe a century

I have put

The dragon to sleep

75. PORTAL IN THE GREEN SKY

Here I am sat
A sky of green opened above me
Saying if you will
Will you love me

Will you examine and chart
This course of shared stars
Above us

Will you hold me
Handle me with care
You have the hands
For that

Can we create
An ethereal space
One we can always
Return to

And one long day

Away

When

That chariot of fire
The one from biblical times
That one that circles and waits
When the end is nigh

Can we leave together
Ride as one into that
Molten light

Become part of
The radiant stars

Can our molecules
Squeeze through
That green expanse together

Can we cool the fire

Pass through that forgotten
Yet ever present
Above us

Portal

In the sky

With love as our fuel
And magic
As our guide

Here I am

Sat

Waiting

For all that

And more

That

Portal

In the sky

76. GOLD ON YOUR UNDERSIDE

You are so precious to me
Like a rock with gold on it's underside
Hidden in a riverbed

Like a magic dew drop
In a mouth of thirst
On the hottest of days

Like the first light beaming
Through a crack in a morning ceiling
Showing a new day is nigh

Like the honey made
By 1000 wild singing bees
In a hive high above
In the canopy of green trees

You my child
Are so loved
And you are so precious to me

Your wings are yours
May you always fly free

Home will always be my heart
When you need me

You are

So precious to me

You are

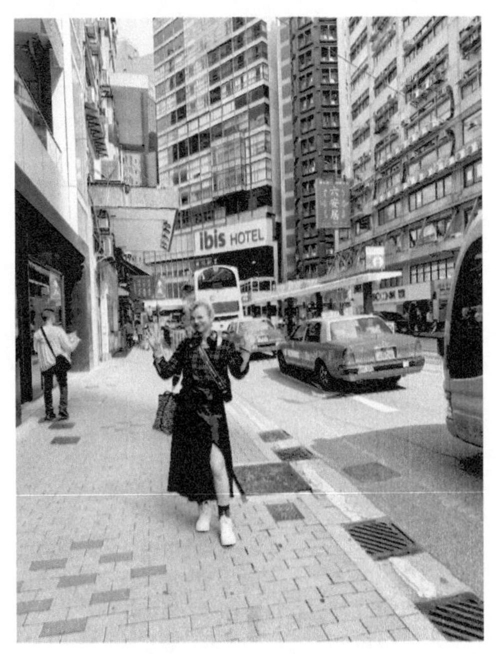
ibis HOTEL
六安居

77. RUMINATION

Yes it is true
The past matters not

Who and how love was
Matters not

I have now
We have now

I feel love from the depth
Of my soul

I do not feel lack
Only joy
Only whole
And two feet
On the ground

And I am so grateful
I want to hug you
With this full cup
And spill out and down
On to your feet and mine

And bless this path we walk on
And for all we have shared
All we know
To be true

No room for languid
Ruminations

But joy
Yes joy

For all and all and all

For this present
And for you

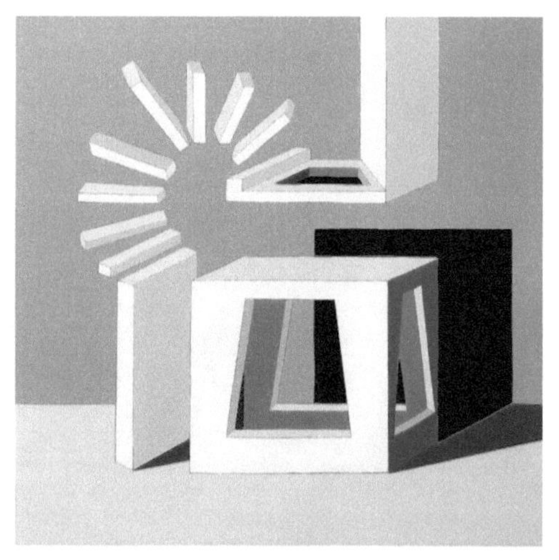

78. QUE SERA SERA

Full stop
Is this the end

Us grinding to a mighty close
After all we have shared
After all this intensity
All this
Blood sweat and tears
After so much
Unavoidable vulnerability

Was it written in the stars
For this to be for a lifetime

Or just a wrenching lesson

I blow a kiss
Into the atmosphere
And I send love

And gratitude
A smattering
An explosion
A gentle wave

All for you
My heart stays open

Que sera sera
Que sera sera

Full stop
Or open door
I am at peace
On either shore

Whatever will be will be

79. SEA ANGEL

The sea angel
Plays
Moves
Weaves
It's way through it's world
Oblivious to it's luminous beauty
It winds through watery ways
Flips
Turns and celebrates

It is free and innocent

It caught my eye
And now I can't unsee it

And you
My child

You

Play
Move
Weave
Your way through this world
Oblivious to your luminous beauty
Winding through watery ways

Flipping
Turning
Celebrating

So free and innocent

My beautiful

Sea angel

Child

80. I LIKE FORESTS

I like forests
And I have decided
It's because
There is power
In their numbers

These parks
With their poisoned edges
With their solitary
Trimmed trees

Domesticated

Like me

Lost their wildness
And their community
Their roots stretch
Underground
But they touch nothing

They curl back
To that place of

Being one

This is not how
It was supposed to be
I don't belong
In a row of planted trees
Neatened with a guided hand

Return me
Please
To the forests
To the running waters
To the bracken broken
And moss cracked rocks

Disturb me
Uproot me
Move me

And plant me
Where I was meant to be

Beside you
In a forest
With the endless air

The storm
The rain
And roots intertwining

Evermore
Together

Evermore

Wild and free
Return me

To me

I like forests
I like trees
I like being

Wild and

Free

81. ONE WHITE OWL

Tears fell for this beautiful small owl
Who collided with the car in front of me
Soft and bleeding
Red on white downy feathers
Nature crushed so often by humans

Of which I am one

And I wept and yet
I remembered too
The circle of life

And how her heart
Could now nurture the earth
And how both could forgive
And expand my and our humanity

And I was reminded
Of the temporal again
And that the owl was not sad

Just moved to another dimension

Like so many things I have lost

We have lost

And in my blurred tears I then let go
Of all I have held on to

My grief for all things unexpressed

And of the earth and the owl
Neither of them

Need me

Yet together there is something ancient
Something remembered
Something sacred

When humans were different
When we cared
And were connected

When to animal and dirt
We felt like family

And so now
In the remembering
And in the letting go

There is more of that wisdom in me
Activated and seen

There is more of what is real
More of what
I was intended to be

More glowing white owl
More animal
More dirt

More of me

Has grieved and is free

And is now buried

Under

The Studio

Tree

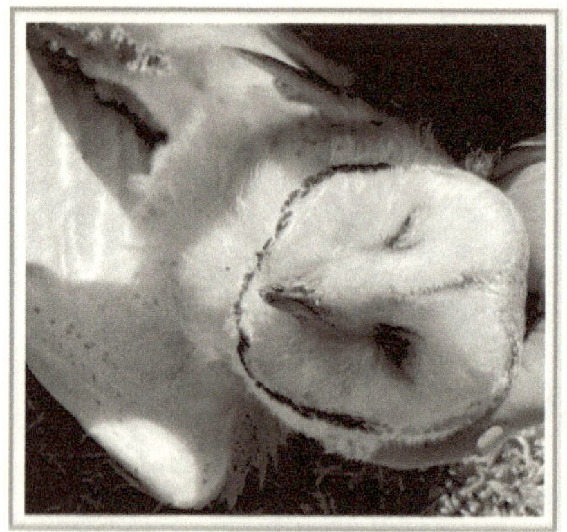

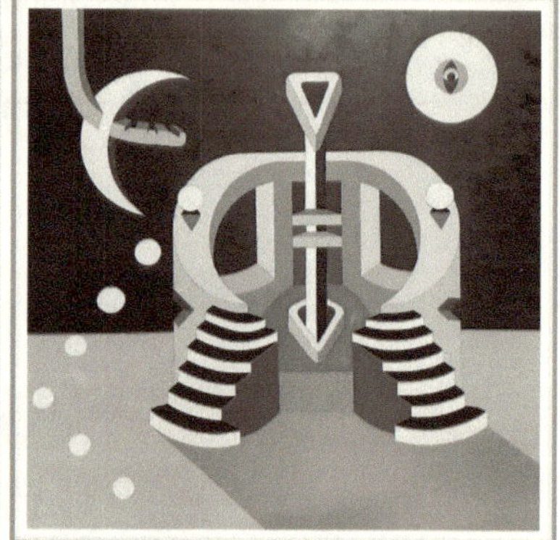

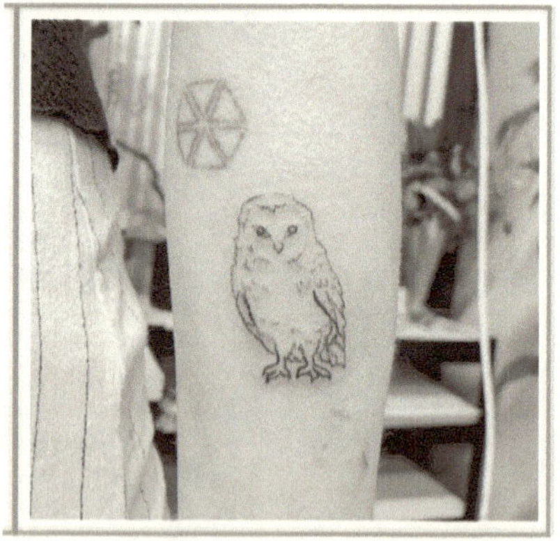

82. I AM THE MUSE

I am the muse

I am the river
I am the rolling stone
I am the mountain
The winding path
The wind

And the sea

I am the muse

And the muse

Is me

83. FAMILY TREE

(ALMA THE OAK)

Put your ear to our tree
If your heart is quiet enough
If you feel beyond your senses

You will hear her song

She draws up
From within the earth
A quiet and powerful melody
The voice of the ancients

Is within her

She breathes and sighs
Her mouth is the wind
She imparts her love
And her wisdom

And her voiceless words say

Slow yourself
Still yourself

In the midst of chaos

Root yourself
Ground yourself

Into this present earth

Put your ear to our tree
If your heart is quiet enough
If you feel beyond your senses

You will hear her song

Listen and wait

Listen long

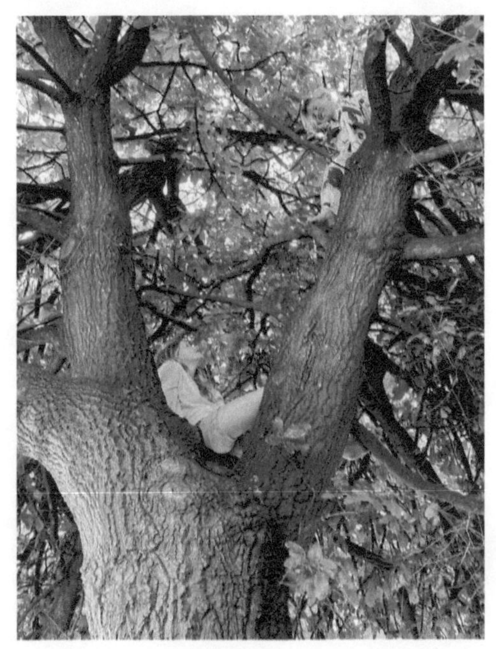

84. THINGS THAT SHATTER

The illusion that love can be

It can shatter like glass in an instant
A one sided side swipe
From an oncoming vehicle
A heart on life support
Fingers raw from the tearing
At the tidal waves of emotion
Holding to the edges of an imaginary boat
That may as well
Be sinking

And then the brakes are slammed
The waves overturn all
And you walk away
You swim to a shore
And you kiss your heart
Weeping and grateful
For it's bravery

Wandering the sand dunes
Wandering the open road
Breathing in the new air
Being completely
Terrifyingly alone

Yet also free

And love no longer an illusion
Pumps inside of your own heart
And gives you your own life

And blood
And marrow
And bone

All back to you
All things new

You
A survivor
A beautiful human
In your own right and time
Ready for anything now
And free
And alone

85. THE PARADOX OF WEIGHTLESSNESS

For I am breathless in my nothingness
Yet the weightless bird can fly
Because of this
The weightlessness

But these small delicate bones
Smash if they touch the ground too soon
The paradox is crushing
When great height meets
A dangerous low

So I ask for the wind to hold me
To keep me abreast a cloudless sky
To whisper to the night air

To envelope me
To surround me
To keep my heart
And keep my life

For my landing to be gentle
For my frame to be protected and held
For the love to be like ever open arms
To a restless babe
Like the ones I have held myself
And raised

That mercy and grace and love
Could and would always be mine
That in my aloneness
I should never be alone

That the heart
Of the universe
Will always be my home
Will always
Be mine to own

For I am breathless
In my nothingness

86. MOULDY CRUMBS

This on my tongue
Literally and metaphorically
When I woke up

I dodged a bullet
Ughh... thank God

I retched and heaved and then
I threw up moldy crumbs
The ones you fed to me

The ones you left in my stomach

My tears I dried then
Slapped on my humble pride
Rescued myself again
Grateful for
The potent reminder
To not lose me

So easily

I went and lay in fields
To look up at the sky
To know
I know
I understand why

A reminder to let go
To be free
To care more
About me

It's easy

If I don't lose sight

Of me

And get distracted by

Mouldy crumbs

87. BOUNDARIES

With all of this interest in the people and the worlds outside of me, I have begun questioning my own boundaries and the rules that have previously kept me safe, or that at least have helped me to be able to maintain some kind of higher ground. A sense of separation and safety.

My own boundaries have helped me to feel autonomous and content within myself, not needing approval or another's love to make me feel ok. If you pay attention, the people around you will mirror to you where you are letting your boundaries be crossed and where they may have ended up being unnecessary walls that keep the right people out.

I have discovered over time that with a commitment to the present moment and by trusting my own intuition and my nervous system, I can be more confident overall and am better able to determine the difference between an unhealthy pushing of my boundaries and the necessary expansion of my comfort zones for growth.

For me a lingering anxiety in my body and a chemical rush are signs I need to pay attention to, as is a persistent lack of peace. The awareness of these signs and other discomforts and the investment in my own autonomy over time has helped me to tune into the still small voice inside of me and it now underpins all I do. It is the voice that I once shut down for so many years when I was younger to remain in unhealthy situations. This new occupation of my body and the listening to it has meant I can now move more freely and confidently in the world. Knowing I will know what I need to know, when I need to know it.

I have learnt these things the hard way and am sharing as I feel discussing boundaries is important for us all.

Remembering:

I can safely own my own boundaries.
I can have boundaries and be loved.
I can have boundaries and be safe.

That if I listen to my intuition, I will always know
When my boundaries are being crossed.

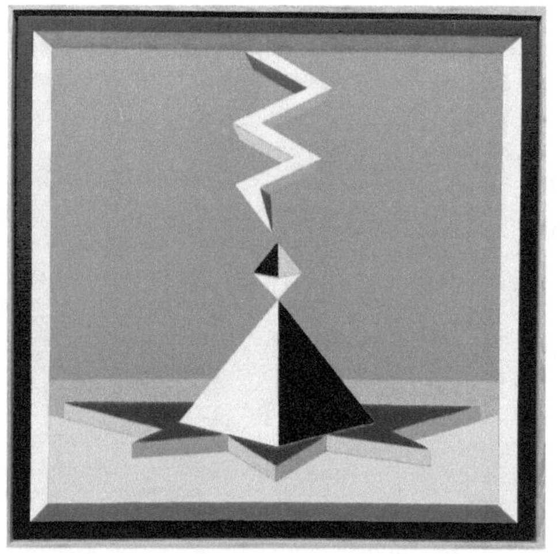

88. SWALLOWING POETRY

Swallowing poetry
Taking it inward
Exchanging it with me

It slips from my brain
To form here in my mouth
Rolls round my tongue

Orders my thoughts
Calms my mind
Circles back
Becomes something else
Helps me make sense

Of all this world around us

I swallow my poetry

89. LUCID

I am becoming more lucid
And luminous
The more I leave
The beaten path

And the less I worry
About a fall
And the valley below

I am a mountain
I am a peak
I have withstood
Hail and rain
And storm

Insult and injury

Escaping always
To a portal

Twas first to hide
But now to see

The opening illuminated

1000 years
Of being me

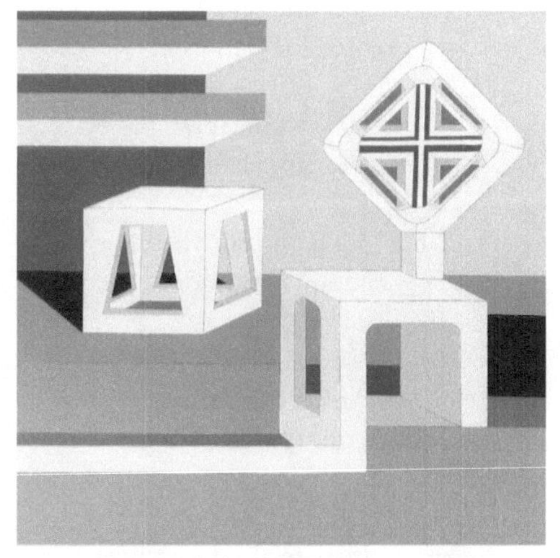

90. BETWEEN THE MOON AND THE SUN

You were on a pedestal
Somewhere between
The Moon and the Sun

I laid my heart on an alter
On a shrine I made
In your honour

Where I worshipped you
Sat in your shadow
Longed for your light

And yet I see now
All my cards laid out

That I am my own world
I contain multitudes

I am my own
Perfect number
That one stands strong
Alone

For an alter can also be a tower
A sacrifice is also a gift

So I draw back
My power

Emit my own light
Draw myself in

And make the Moon and the Sun

My very own again

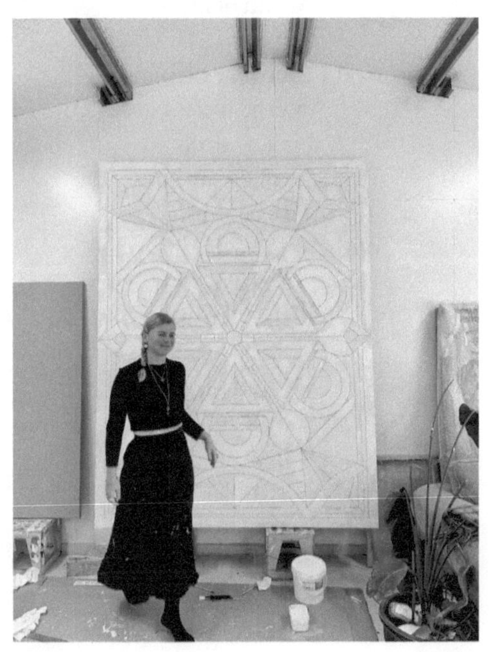

91. LIKE A SPEEDING TRAIN

Like a speeding train
My life roars on
Ahead of me

And I count my blessings
And the nights
I get to sleep
Stacked like sardines
In a bed
With my kids and my cats
Awake
While they are asleep

Arms and legs
Tangled all around me

And I breathe this love
This fleeting melancholy
That is time passing by

Far too quickly

Like a speeding train
My life roars on

Ahead of me

92. DECISIONS

All the decisions you don't make
Are the decisions you do make

The things you let slide that slide
The words you keep inside

Taking no action
Is an action

Action without intention
Is an action

Laziness or blind stupid faith
Path of least resistance
Passiveness
Wisdom or foolishness in spades

Sometimes I can't decide

Decide

Yet I know this

All the decisions you don't make
Are the decisions you do make

So

What will you decide

Or not decide

93. HIDING IN ART

You can hide in art

Make a whole world there
Disassociate and dream

Live in your own fantasy
Bubbles of reality

Untouched by the
Day to day

Pains and heartaches

Or are they

Pains and heartaches

If you can create from them

You can hide in art
Make a whole life there
Associate and elevate
No one can touch
Or take away

Your home there

Or can they

You can hide in art

94. ALEX

One day you woke up
Buttoned your shirt
Cleaned your teeth

Said toodle-oo

One day you
You went on your way
And never knew

It was to be your last

One day I kissed
Your quiet cheek
And I said goodbye

Said toodle-oo

One day
An ordinary
But not
Ordinary

Day

So

Love all the days
In all the ways

And

Love like it
Just may be

Your last

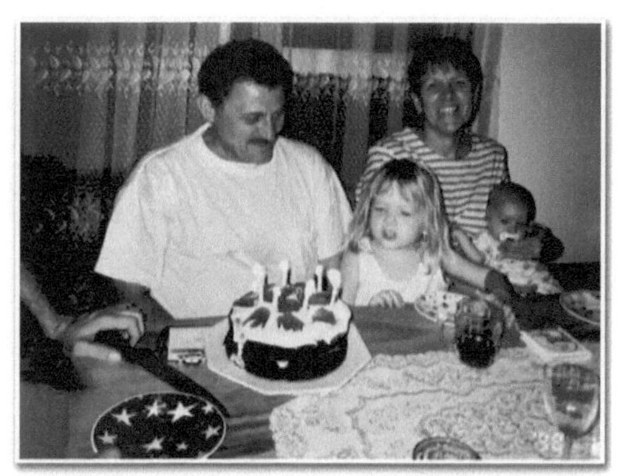

95. MOTHER OWL

Mother Owl
Swoops to my heart
Lets herself in
Brings her wisdom
Places it
Under my skin

Mother Owl
Sharpens my eyes
Helps me see clearly
My skin
Her disguise

Mother Owl
Her soft downy feathers
Razor-sharp beak
She is fearless

She is wise

Mother Owl
Swoops to my heart
Let's herself in
Brings her wisdom

Places it

Under my skin

Thank you Mother Owl

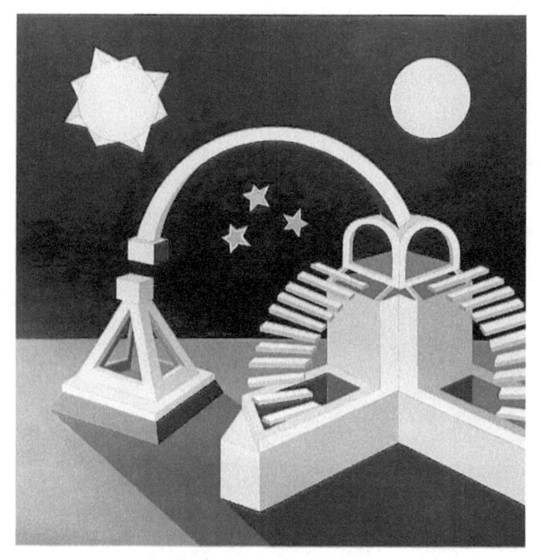

96. CLOUD SPIRIT

Baby cloud
All alone

But a puff
A breath

Is it you
In a moment

Suspended
In the air

A reminder
You are here

You are there

Baby cloud
But a memory

Without
A care

Without
A home

Always here
Always there

Baby cloud

Of the air

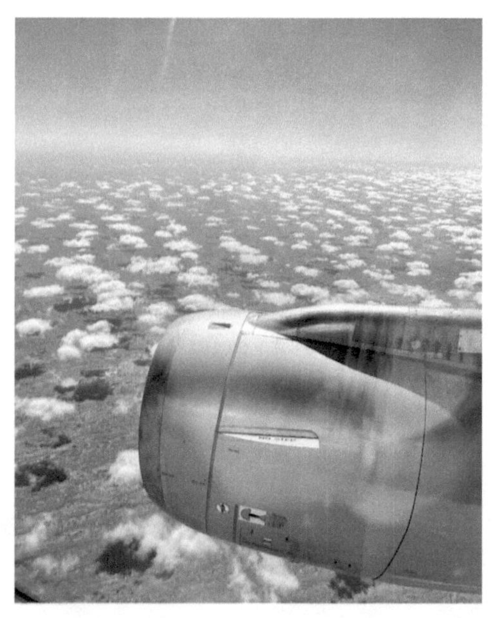

97. BANK OF TIME

Bank of time
I keep withdrawing from

Can't credit
Only debit from you
Each minute passes
In a joy
Or a melancholy
Moment

I feel you
Like air
On my cheek
A memory

One time took

And yet what newness
Will time bring
What sweetness
In numbers
May lay ahead

For I see now
Though I can't see it
Can only see
A balance sheet
That had you

Written on it

One that time took

And time

Gave away

98. SECOND SKINS

I do not want to shed this skin
Said the snake
It is too difficult
I am afraid

Yet

I am stifled
I am uncomfortable

But dear snake I say
What choice do you have

You shed it now
Or you stagnate in it

And then you die

You must do the hard thing
You must take the time
To wrestle with the past
To struggle

To try

To work yourself free

To rise to new life

To once again

Thrive

You will have new skin again

In time

Thank God for

Second Skins

Second Skins

99. WE LEAVE ONLY AIR

I want to fall into you
Like one falls into a cloud
A sweet song
A melody
I want to fall some place
No one has ever yet been
A path somehow
Revealing itself
Leaving only air
In our wake

I want to lie with you
Under the bluest of skies
Closing my eyes
Feeling the kisses
Of sun and butterflies
On our cheeks

I want to lie with you
And disappear
For a time
Into a dream
One with endless nights
And angels white winged

I want to lie with you
On a bed in the stars
Our hearts
Pressed together
Our blood in sync

Our time eternal
Our love eternal

Tis all

Tis everything

We leave only air

100. ONLY MONKS

Only monks get to grieve in silence

The rest of us see our tears
Fall into sinks full of dishes
Or patted up from spreadsheets

We hold them back at checkouts
Or dry them between stops
In the busy morning traffic
We blow our kisses to shadows
We find form in the thinnest air
We wait until the shower is perfect
Let our sadness fall there

We dive into an icy ocean
Where the salt meets the salt
And nobody is there to care
We wish for time to stop
And that it wasn't now

One
Two
Eight
Ten days

Since you passed away
Knowing the time
Is supposed to mean
It's starting to feel ok

Only monks get to grieve in silence

I still need to cook a decent dinner
I need to kiss small heads
And tell them about the place
Where you went and
In which you now wait

Only monks get to grieve in silence

But then all the silence
In the world right now

Would not make this feel better
Would not have made you better

Would not have made any difference
Would not have given you

Another breath

Won't bring you back again

Now all that can be done
Is to think of that monk

And that acceptance
And that expansion

To acknowledge as he does
That life is life
In all its highs and lows
All experience is equal

Tis bittersweet and tis beautiful

That without death would we truly live

Without this bookmark in time
This brief circle of earthly eternity
Appreciate life and love

For what it truly is

Only monks get to grieve in silence

101. RUBY

Ruby girl

We are connected
Not only by love
My babies
And you

You

Carry the same blood
The same DNA
Flows through

All three of your veins

Ruby girl

May the world
We share
Always be small
Always be kind

To you

You will forever

Have a seat
At my table
And a place
In my heart

You will always and forever

Be so very

Very

Loved

102. STEPHEN

I cooked in your kitchen
Put your chilli flakes on my dinner
Tonight

Drove your car with fresh bills
Stuffed
In the glovebox

Ones you won't be paying

Brushed my teeth
In your sink

Sat on your lounge
Played with your dog

Cried tears by your pool
My reflection reflecting
The full Moon

And you

Both looking down

At me

Gazing at the stars
Grieving for the fact
That everyday

Takes you

One more

Step

Further

Away

Your fridge emptied
Your bills paid

Someone else
Brushing their teeth

In your sink

Slowly you
From systems erased
Left only

In memories
And in minds

And in hearts like mine

Hearts that you did not mean to

By leaving so early

Break

103. BEREFT

I have been
Run through
Done through
Flattened bulldozed
Done for
Done in
Run out of
My sense of self
Lost in you
Like I always was

Yet I still feel guilty
Of all I am
Not grateful for
A roof over my head
Not living in a war
Children wrapped around me
As I lay in my bed

Yet in the midst of all of this
Being broken
Of all being lost

I cling to you still
Like I always did

For far below my skin
You were always there
All the you that you were

Good and bad
Lost and found

And I wish I had given you more

That last drop of blood
I had left
I wish I had shared
But I didn't

I needed that one

For myself

And so
Here I am

A flattened plain
A vast space
Uninhabited
Except for memories
And ghosts

And dreams I had to let go

I saved myself
I could not save us both

So all I can do
Is grieve what you lost

What I lost
What everyone who loves you

Lost

And let myself be

Flattened
Bereft
Bulldozed
Done in
Done for

Without you

104. WOMB OF THE MOON

I was held
In the womb
Of the Moon

Long before
I met a mother

Long before
I loved another

I was held
In the womb
Of the Moon

I felt the glow within
I felt the glow without

A small spark I was

Waiting to be lit
With the fire
Of my birth

So when my
Heart is done here
My body done here

I will return

To be held
In the womb
Of the Moon

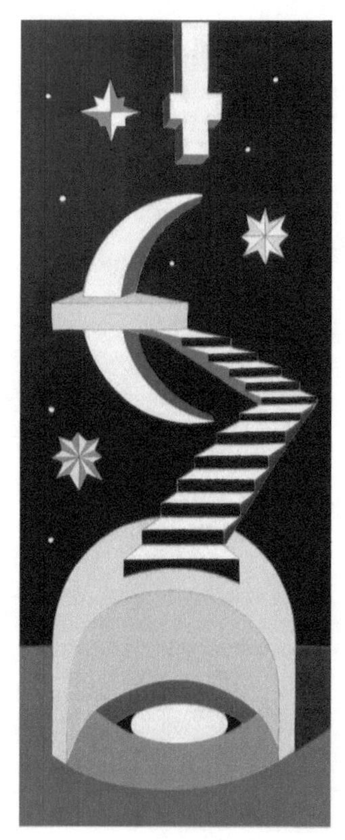

105. FEED MYSELF FULL

All you ever have given to me
All your heart had to give
Was crumbs and dry bones

My heart had been cut
Torn and bleeding
I never wanted you more

Or needed you more

This was the time
To let the heavens open
To let your rains pour

But you just left me empty
And that being a feeling
So familiar

I was full on nothing

Until I realized
Had an epiphany

Of how much I have survived alone
That I can feed myself
Both crumbs and bones

And that this was why
We had ended
In the first place

And why I should close my heart
And move on

Feed myself full
Leave the table
You left laid
Bare

106. NOTHING IS NEW

Everything has been done
There is no human feeling new
No pain not yet felt
No loss is ever just one

There is no joy
Or ecstasy nor hope
Nor woe
No care nor concern

Nothing is new
Under the sun

We are all just
Living now
Under this one

We all fail
We all pretend
We all stand at times
On shaky shaky

Ground

Life in its seasons
Repairs challenges
Breaks and mends
The circle continues

Again and again

I look above the crowd
The often empty words
And in silence I wonder

What all the noise is for

How do I pare back
Scrape back
Take back
It all to the core

How do I separate and burn
The things that
Do not matter

Anymore

For where there is breath
There is one day death
Where there is life
There is sure to be love

Where there is youth
There is age
And so on and so forth

And I want to live my fullest
And my truest
And my rawest
And my most real self

All my days
Under this sun
This one and only

Sun

Where nothing is new

107. GO WHERE THE LOVE IS

Go where the love is
Where you are wanted

Do not put

Your pearls

Before swine

Do not sell your soul
For those who would

Put it aside

Go where the love is
Where you are wanted

Do not put your heart

Out to dry

Find your people
Find your tribe

Love those who love you

And then

Love them

Hard

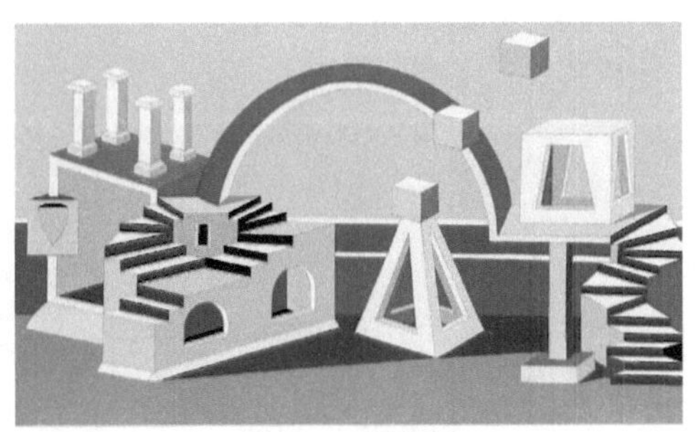

108. CAN'T FORCE A HEART

You cannot make a heart go
Where it does not want

To go

You can't force it

Push it
Hold it

When it comes to hearts
When they want to go
You must let them go

Liking forcing a horse

To water

Like shoving arithmetic

Down a throat

When a heart is gone

It is gone

Done and gone

And all that is left
Is to let go

Let go
Let go
Let go

And if it returns
It returns
On its own

109. ADVENTURER OF OLD

Like an adventurer of old
Seas crossed
Storms endured
Waves dumped
Heart fatigued

I feel I have arrived
On the most beautiful
Of foreign shores
Shade plentiful
Abundant everything

My head resting
On cool white sand
My heart softened
By the beauty
Of this new land

Like an adventurer of old
Nothing was guaranteed
Following only a promise
A hunch
A fool's dream

I feel I have arrived
At a place only the brave get to be
Only the followers
Of stars and signs
Get to see

The paradise that is
The adventurers reward
For it's true
We all know it to be
That fortune has always
Favoured the bold
And now
Just now
It has favoured

Me

110. WE WALK THE MOUNTAIN

I take my pain
To the Mountain
And I walk with it

Letting it lag behind

Letting it sink
Below my heart
Fall to my feet

The higher I climb
The further I go
The freer I feel

Your ghost
Your memory
Is gentler here

So I take my pain

I take your ghost
And together

We walk the Mountain

And gratitude for this relief
Overwhelms me
And love floods me

And I return new
To the hum
Of the common place

The everyday

That is my life
My day changed
Altered and new

I take my pain
To the Mountain
And I walk with it

And I walk with you

III. CLOSE TO THE SHORE

Are you any closer to the shore

I asked her

Can your hear the gulls
The waves soft
Lapping a sandy stretch

The smell of a cool forest
You could sleep there
Safe enveloped

Are you any closer to the shore

Or do dark clouds still loom
Is your boat still
Ravaged and threatened

Is dry land but a dream
The sea so huge
Expansive overwhelming

This journey of 1000 miles
999 of them will have you
Feeling lost

So

Hold your face high
Then the torrid force of the deep
Will only drive you forward

Closer to that shore
That bay
That place of peace

Of rainless
Windless
Breathless
Skies

Where the heart exhales
The body heaves
All trace
Of past travails

Gone

You are so close to the shore
You are so close to the shore

You are so close

To the shore

I told her

Hold on
Head high

You are so close

To the shore

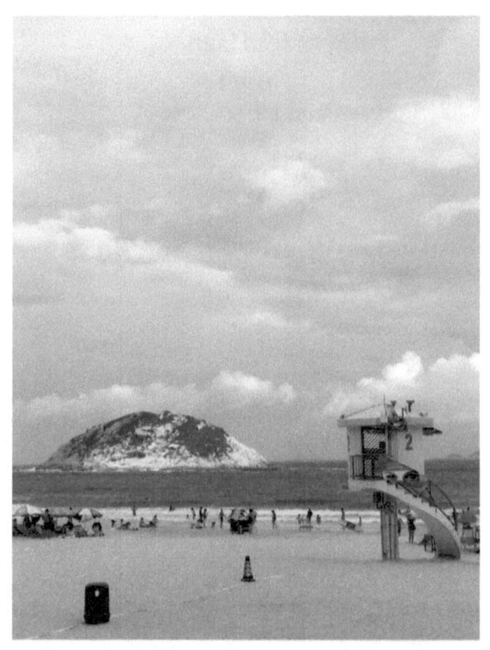

2

112. CROSSROADS

My childhood mind
Never imagined
The choices
Adult me
Would have to make

The crossroads
I sit at every day

No decision
Being a decision

Of itself

Empowered
Dis empowered

Decisive
Indecisive

I weave
I turn
And I loop back
To the place I started

Not a crossroad
But a rollercoaster

A crossroad
With an ever-widening center

A crossroad
Like a spinning wheel

With all its choices

Once upon a time
All I ever wanted

Was

Fresh cool air
Cash for food
Wine and bills

Peace
Quiet
Safety

And the love of you

When did it all become

So grey

So murky

So up and so down

Is this an answer

In itself

If you don't know

Does that make you sure

Is that the end

Of the crossroad

113. NO RECEPTION

No reception
Equals

No

Self-deception

I sit with
Myself
And myself

Alone

No salvation
To be found
In the
Comfort

Of my

Phone

114. THE BEYOND

You set forth

Returned from whence you started

Went beyond this earth

You went and joined

The secret life

Of stars

Forever

Departed

Leaving me

Broken

And

Broken

Hearted

115. SECRET LIFE OF STARS

So often I wonder
About the secret life of stars

Unreachable
Ever present
Visible
Invisible

Lost from a mother
Found by another

Magnificent
Common
Luminous
Adored

Set apart
Untouchable

Existing in dreams
Present in myths
Fantasies
And illusions

I am forever drawn
Gazing
Wishing
Seeing lost loves

Twinkling
Far above

All I can do is wonder
About the
Secret life

Of stars

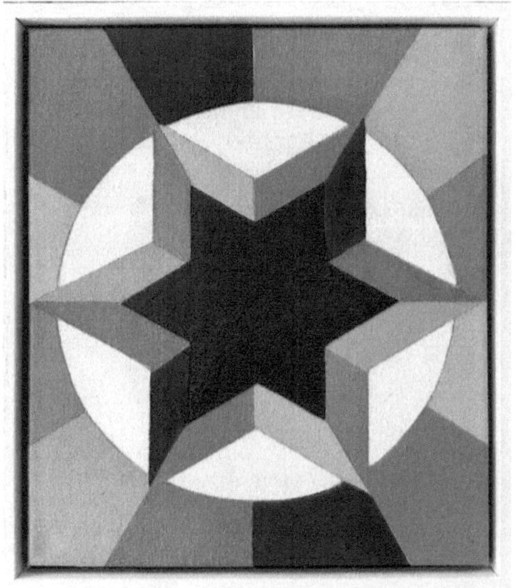

116. MAMA

I am one blessed Mama

Five children
Five anchors
Five teachers

Five people to hug
To hold in my heart

To learn of the meaning of Mama love

Five mirrors
Five arrows
Five firecrackers

Five ways
My heart beats and breaks

Five prayers
To five angels

Five people to miss

Five people

To forever be proud of
To make a life for and because of

Five people to watch grow
Five amazing humans

Gifted to me

I am one blessed Mama
Please give me

Grace
Wisdom
Strength

To be the Mama
They need

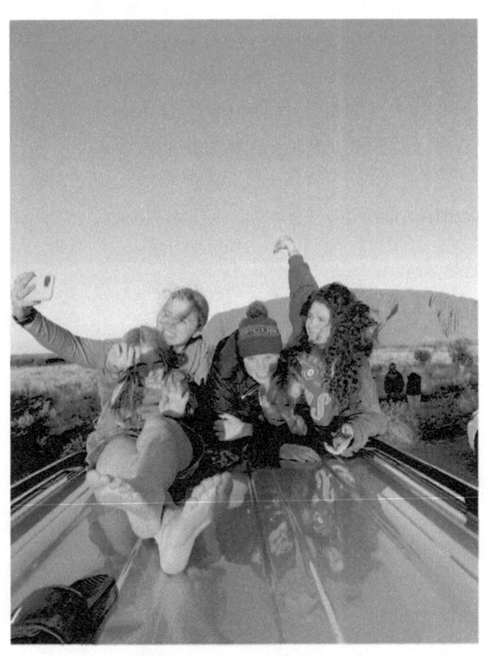

117. WORTHY OF REST

Rest
Rest
Rest

Don't ever forget
No matter where you are at
Or where you have been
That you are made of stardust

Remember the world beyond the day to day
The perspective of infinity
Making everything feel

More than ok

Fold your hands
Soften your breath
There is always tomorrow
Wings to outstretch

But for this one minute

Slow down and rest
You are worthy of this

Rest
Rest
Rest

118. SEASONS

Of course I have moments when I falter, but I sense this quickly these days and can return to the trust that everything I need will come to me when I need it. I soften more easily than ever into the seasons. To the ebbs and flows of life.

I remind myself that everything I am experiencing is for my greater good and for the good of those around me. That the desires of my heart and all that aligns with what I have asked for, is coming to me, and in a way, it is already here in its unfolding. That the present season is the season.

I have come to understand that to achieve my desires, I must also be a container able to hold them. This is the gap between where I am and where I want to be. I need to be able to hold a greater capacity myself if I wish to have a greater capacity in the world.

In this way, my desires are in keeping with what I am a match to.

So, in the various seasons of life, we are being prepared for the next. My job, as I see it, is to be as fully myself as I can be; in this way, I can see where my own cracks and fault lines are, where I still have work to do. As it is in the seasons of the natural world, the cycle is a loop, it is a continuous circle, and growth is not linear.

If you are reading this, my hope is that via my works you will see the world in a new way. That you will be kinder to yourself and feel more connected via my vulnerability. That you will see everything happening in your own life as an opportunity for your soul's growth. That you will feel braver and less afraid. That it will be with new eyes you will view yourself and your experiences. That you will become more aware of your own filters and how they may be affecting how you see and, therefore, how you show up in the world.

That you will trust the season you are in and take the lessons being presented to you, with grace, ease and surrender.

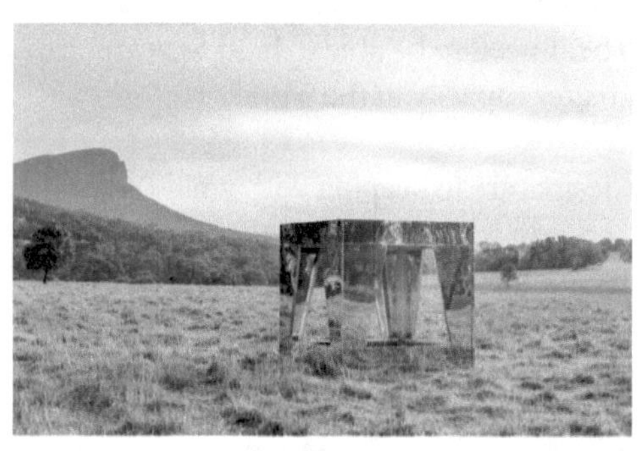

119. BREAD AND HONEY

I baked you into bread
And I slathered you
With honey

I called you to me
Then I put you into

My body

And we became

One and the same

Food and flesh

Before I was just

One mortal
On the floor

But now together
We are a single
Full bodied

Force

Bread
Honey

Body

More

120. THE TRICK

The trick is

As I see it

Is to not be
So let go
So fallen apart
That the pieces
Can't be
Sewn back
Together

Later

After the storm
After the
Aftermath

That you
Are not like
The rag doll
With parts too worn

Too thread bare
To replace

This is the trick

As I see it

How to live and to last

121. PADDOCKS

It was very late one night that I drove past a huge fire in a paddock on my way home from the city. A farmer burning off waste in the middle of nowhere. I stopped to watch it awhile, as it made me think of something that had been on my mind. Fire is such a powerful metaphor for change, for clarification. Forced new beginnings. Fire is a vivid reminder that there are times when things have to be burned away.

So, I asked myself then, and I ask you now. What doesn't serve you anymore? Because what got you to this point might not necessarily be what you need to get you to where you are going next.

Also, to have light, you have to have fire. Something has to burn to give.

My life has changed so much, and yet it needs to keep evolving. So much has fallen away. I feel forever changed. It's been hard to stop and face myself sometimes. To ask questions about myself and how authentically I am showing up in the world, to think about my art and who I am making it for. Hard questions about the muse, about my voice and what it is I have to share. About me as a person, and how I want to be here, there and everywhere. To always be true to myself.

Everything has a time and a season, and if you are in fire season, please know you are not alone. We are all, to a degree, in a time of uncertainty and rapid change. We are going through a collective fire. But in a way, haven't we humans always been?

There is a light coming through, however. I can feel that too in my own life. Hold on and be strong. Live in the light of the fire and equally fix your eyes on the light at the end of the tunnel.

Growth, change and expansion are always uncomfortable. Yet the alternative, stagnation, is equally difficult, and growth leads somewhere, stagnation leads nowhere. Just death to parts of self. That's the truth of it.

Also, sometimes you don't choose the fire; it chooses you, and you get thrown into it.

If you needed to hear this just now. If this is you, I am sending love. Remember the darkest of night is the hour before dawn. That light and dark exist in polarity. You can't have one without the other,

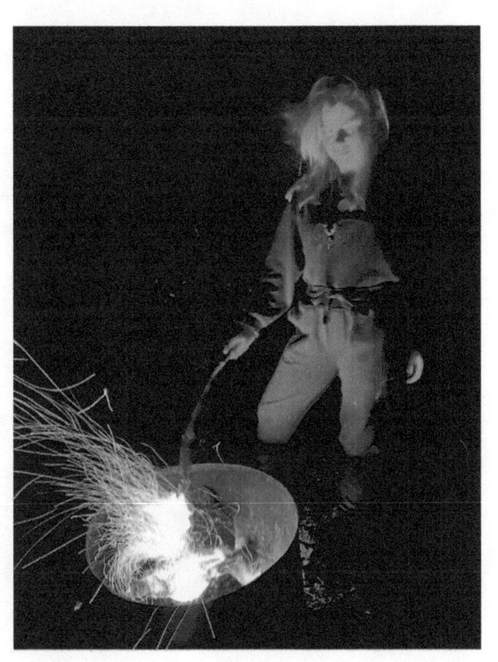

122. MAGIC WANDS

The invitation to more
The magic wand
You hold to me

Curling with light
And promise

Things I don't trust

But should

And I wish I could

Somehow

I manage to say

Don't give up on me

Don't leave me

Keep your heart open

Leave the light on

For me

Hold that magic wand

Close

Just hold me

123. THE PENDULUM

The pendulum
Swings between
Feeling and freezing
Freezing and feeling

No diving here
No leaping
Jumping
Only sliding slowly
Stretching out a finger
A limb
A slow
Crawl
Closer
To the center of things
And to you
The center being warm
Expanded
And expanding

A cloud
Heavy with rain
Bursts bringing fresh earth
A heart
A light
A long refrain

And here now
Just a weight

And a pendulum
Swinging between
Feeling and freezing
Freezing and feeling

And back to the beginning
It all starts again

More or less

One and the same
The pendulum swings
Again and again

124. NO ACE

I could stop here
Lay my head
And my hat here

Put my shoes
Under the bed here

But what of fate
This hand
Half dealt

This hand missing
A winning card

An ace

No resting head
No shared bed

Move on
Move on

Roll the dice

Once more

Move on
Move on

125. FLIES BUZZ ROUND EMPTY CUPS

The flies buzz today
Signaling the departure of magic

In the real world there is a corpse
There was a dagger

No dance left only one foot
On the grave

The song sung
The melody now
Impossible to remember

The luminous Moon
Replaced by a beating Sun
The lips with shallow words
From passers by

Now non-participants
Of your life
Empty of glow
Everything now just sacrifice

I know
I have been down this street
Laid on this ruined grass

I know it's familiar smell

Don't need a dream or a premonition
To tell me how this will end

It's a scene I know well

Threading through my mind
Are the ways to return to a path
Well trod
To a better place

One in my mind
Where I can go
To safety and higher ground
I can rest and wait it out
Wait for the ache to pass

Wait

For my spine to shiver again
And the blanket of light
To return to envelope me

I align with the luminous moon
The dagger less dance
The melody of MY magic

Returns

A reminder for me to be free
To create my own wonderland

Not rely on on the one
Projected on and around

Me

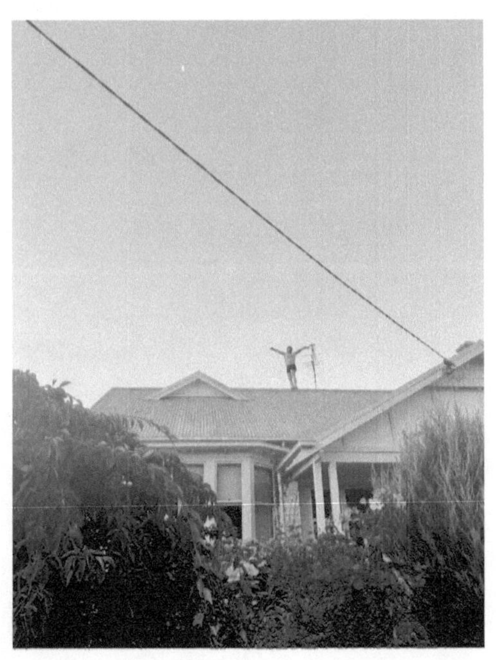

126. NO WORDS

Stuff me full of words

Ram them

Down

My throat

This holy

Unholy

Dialogue

Fill me

Till I choke

For I have words

Until

I have

No words

127. NOTES FROM NEVERLAND

Dragged down from dreams
Never kicking or screaming
Tugged by the tail into this realm

Brought to light
Brought to life

From the underbelly of an unknown whale
To the wings of a familiar white owl
Lifted by a double Pegasus

A new view of this world

Here come the words
Here come the words

Little pictures themselves form
Little structures beam down
The words have worlds now

Protected by the teeth of my friend the tiger
The snarl of my brother the wolf
The subtle moves of a swan sister
The forms that inhabit this earth
Everything aligns to hold space until

Little lands appear then to give worlds
To the words from Neverland
To give homes to new stories
To new ideas
New ways of being

Intertwining stairs form now
Mirrors and doors appear

The windows and arches of my childhood
Sacred places
My dreams long held them dear

All and everything becomes this now
An ethereal landscape

All that is the Neverland of my mind
And the Neverland of yours
This how the everything forms
And this is how new worlds

Are born

128. THIS BLOODY BEAT

I open my mouth
Bare my teeth
Stretch my arm
Down my throat

Squeeze my heart

Feel it's blood

Fresh

Squelching through
Ramming every
Distant vein
Artery

My fingertips

Manual feeling
Auto override
Pumping now
Into overtime

I open my mouth
Bare my teeth
Stretch my arm
Down my throat

Yes

My chest still heaves
I can feel my heart
In my hand
This bloody beat

This is proof

I am alive

You have not taken me out

(Yet)

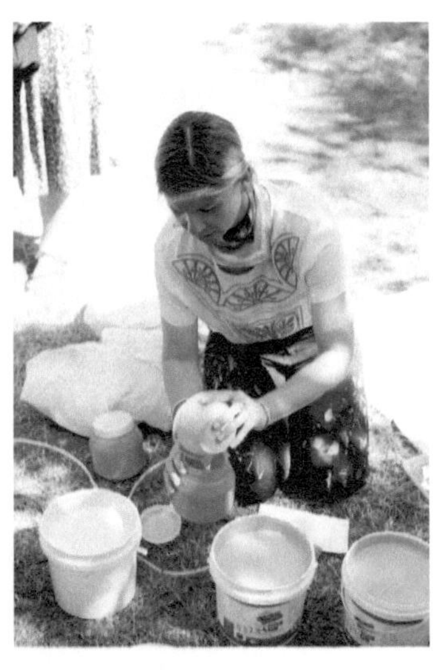 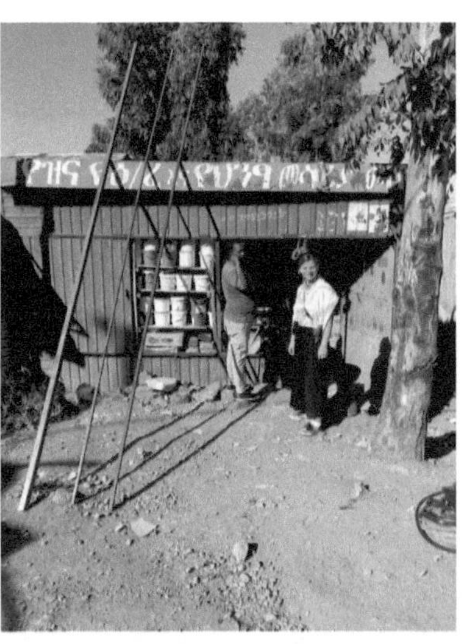

129. TIME

If you really think about time and think of it as the thread which underpins our entire human existence. Time is everything. Everything time gives, it also takes away.

If you think of time on a global scale, in the context of the rising and setting of the sun, then you get the feeling that our lives are actually just one long day. If you take out the sunrise and sunset. We humans compartmentalise time like this; it is how we have chosen to perceive it and break it down. In this way it makes sense to us.

So, when one is pinned to a singular location, time feels organised and routined, a day following a night, again and again. My travels over time, however, have changed how I feel about time and my notion of it. Global time changes, hours back and forward, speaking to people who are waking, while I am preparing for bed. Sleeping while others are working. Twenty-four-hour time, awoke in me the notion of shared time in motion, not the separate days it had once seemed to be for me.

Time is, therefore, one of the human containers I have explored within my work. I feel an endless curiosity around it. I have used my geometric and architectural devices, portals and stairs to create narratives around time to explore this fascination. Some of the perspectives which affect time that I have examined are: time and love, time and love lost, time and loss, time past, time present, lost time, and time and distance.

Time influences everything.

Also, another thing about time, if you have a painting of mine on your wall, or any of my art, then you have captured my time forever on a surface.

Art making is the ultimate exchange of time, creating things that may well outlive you. One of my favourite uses of time.

130. AMOR FATI

(Love your fate)

Fates forever intersecting
At a rate
We cannot calculate

You can dig around asking questions

How
Why
When
Where

But

These fault lines in time
We have no answers for
Just blind faith

Amor fati

Cracks and shifts
Doors shutting and closing
Hearts opening
Five seconds before

You walk on by

Or

You stop and say

Hi and hello
How are you
Where did you come from

So I trust what I see
My eyes reveal
The track and path
The route meant for me

And with an omnipresent
Otherness sometimes
In my dreams I look down
Surveying my life

Considering this and that
Considering my own
Misguided
But guided steps

Plans

The ones that led
Me to you

Or away from you

Our fates once
Like all of them
Crossed

Lines and paths shared
Human journeys and stories
Acts on a common stage
Endings and openings

Fates forever intersecting
At a rate
We cannot calculate

These fault lines
In time
Not fault lines
At all

All divine
All universal
All yours
All mine
Unseen hands
In operation

For all time
Amor fati

You are yours

And I am mine

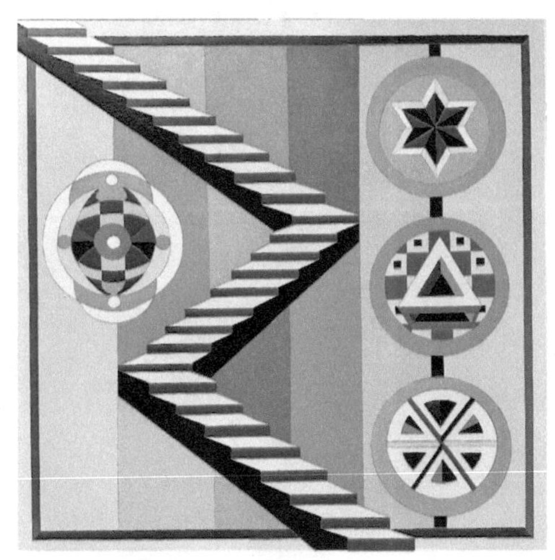

131. TUNISIA I

Being propelled forward towards
Something I have no idea about
No construct of what to expect

I feel the adrenaline of it

The shiver in my shoulders
The sleepless anticipation

Being brave brings so much
New flow and new creation

More life more material

Curiosity equals

Art

Curiosity equals

Living

132. TUNISIA II

Lost taxi
No data
Thumbs up
No English
Stray dogs
Bark and chase us
20-pound tip
Because he is angry
And I have no local
Currency

Just the beginning

To be adrift
But not
Is to see
And to see
Is to expand

Into

The more

More more more
That is available

Freely

Just outside of ones

Comfort zone

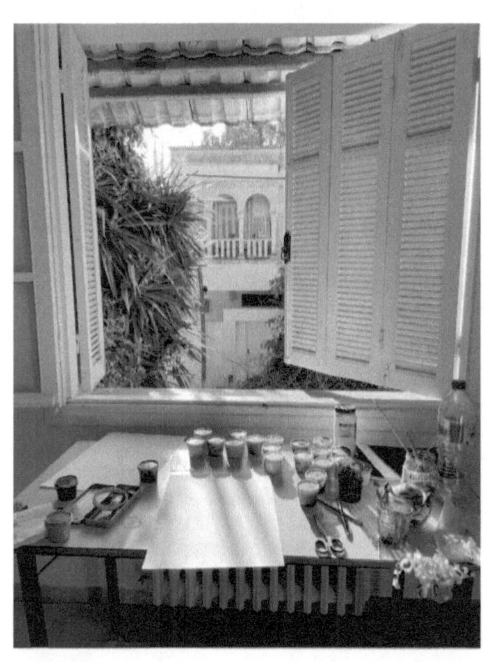

133. FORK IN THE ROAD

Sometimes I wake
At the wrong time of night
With a life on my mind

That feels somehow
Like it should have been mine
A lump in my throat

Rises

And I wonder
If it's not the case
That at some point

Long ago

I missed that fork in the road
Sailed right past it
The one where I chose you
And you chose me

To another
Not quite so right

Place

And that somehow now
I have missed
The love of my

Destiny

And now I must wait
Live out this life

Alone

Live with the wondering
If I am never quite where
And with whom I

Belong

134. DANCE OF FIRE

(FILM NARRATIVE)

We put this fire out
Clear the ash pit

All trace of it
You and I
Are gone

The storm of the heart
Breath of life
Divine in the present
Yet lost
In the sands of time

To burn and race through
The blood
The intensity
Of heat beat and movement

The dance of fire
Is the oldest of arts
The original wordless
Universal

Language

This trance of body
Yours and mine
Consuming a moment
Heaven existing

In the present

And yet

Sometimes

Often

I wish I could be
Stripped of this energy

My melancholy heart asks
Why this heat and smoke
Why were sparks gifted

To me

My fingers are hot
And ignite all I see

This

This storm of ideas
Moving me so quickly
Through life
This relentless dance

Within my head
And in my heart

My feet keeping my own beat
Often a lonely beat
To my own internal

Drum

This life oft not an easy one
Dancing on coals till

Last light

Is all I have
All we have
All humanity has

And this

The most alive
Thread of cells
That lives in me

My gift
And
My legacy

Stay then till the dawn
Till this the last of the light

Then

Then

No fire
No moon
No breath
No body
No heat

No heart

The end was always nigh
Now it is imminent

We put this fire out
Clear the ash pit

All trace of it
The fire
Of you
And I

Are gone

Like the fires before us

And the fires

Yet

To come

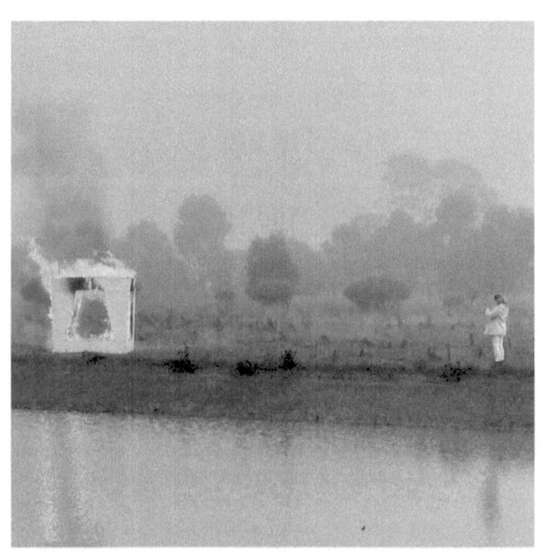

135. A FISH IN A TREE

A fish in a tree
Was how she described me

So I purchased a bowl
Filled it with water
Reeds
Rocks
And a filter

Then I took a ladder
Climbed way up high
Put the bowl in the tree
Close to the sky

And although
It is not that easy

I am not that free

I'm happy you see
Cos now I can be

A

Fish

In

A

Tree

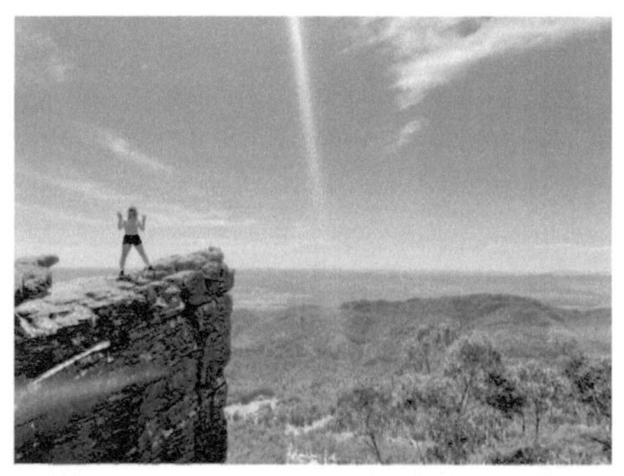

136. LAST SCHOOL BAG

I know that one day this all ends
Last school bag dropped on the floor
For one last

Time

Last squeals from the backyard
Half joy
Half madness
Terrorising
Peaceful
Suburban
Sundowns

Last times I say pick this and that up
Pull apart a scrap
Tuck you all in at night
All of us weary
But my weariness

In the bones

Last time I wash your hair
Brush your hair
Your teeth
Put on your coat
Tie your shoes

Dry your baby tears
Have you sleep on my chest
Feed from my breast

Wipe your face
Wipe your knee

Put a Band-Aid on
An invisible scratch

Last times
For Lego an endless mess
And Weetbix dried
On my kitchen bench

Last times
Last times

How quickly these
Last times become

Last times

Then I say

Hey

Come

Come back
Come visit me
Bring your noise
Your jovial youth
Your energy

Come shake rooms
Unbalancing fine things
Things I once tried to collect
Too soon
Before my house
And you
Were ready

Come

Come

Stay with me
Let me feed you
Love you
Remember you
As your were
Hold you
As you are
Now
Ever my child

Ever the fruit of my womb

Know that you were
The greatest gift
That life
Ever
Gave me

You
You
You
You

And

You

All of you

Come back and come home

Anytime

137. HELD BY THE EVERLASTING EYE

I have left the path of the known
There is no one to follow
No book to read
No guru to light the way

No guide
No map or talisman

Only my heart and my legs
My eyes and my ears
My dreams and ideas

I trust that I am held
Looked after
Invisible forces around and above
Guided by love
I will always have

Enough

This path
Has no end
No fear

If

You cannot die
You cannot lose

This revelation

It is mine

Mine
Mine
As I am

Mine

Held by an everlasting eye
An everlasting arm

I am mine

138. RIDERS IN THE NIGHT SKY

There was a cloud in the night sky
That looked like a horse
And a rider
Leaping forth
Into the abyss
Of that perfect Moon-lit

Distance

And I wanted to feel more
Than I did
In that moment
I wanted a sign
A flag
An epiphany

To tell me
How to be me

But like that cloud
I too hesitate
I am caught mid air
Fist and chin high
Just holding on

Frozen in time

Waiting for wind perhaps
Or rain
Or some other holy
Celestial becoming
To move me forward
Move me on

To tell me
How to be me
How to be free

Again

139. NER THE TWAIN SHALL MEET

You retreat to your corner in skin
Skin I am not welcome in
And I to mine
In broken sadness
I can't cross over to you
And you can't come to me
Ner the twain shall meet

No words enough
No mutual language
To even begin with
We lick our wounds

Individually
Separately
Collectively
Lie in respective beds
Sit as foreigners at tables
In familiar
Yet entirely uncharted
Territory

Wondering what
The point of it all was
This lesson in love and loss
A dream unattainable
In fleshy physicality
Everything invisible

Now visible

The inside of a blocked artery

Hearts and blood
Just out of reach
Under an unreachable
Unseen surface

So

You retreat to your corner
And I retreat to mine
In skin that
Without you

I wish was not mine

140. THINGS ON WINGS

I went to write about a thing
But the muse
Sent another

What was truly laying
Underneath
My skin

Came forth
Dragged out
On its wing

I went to write about a thing
But the muse

Sent another

141. MAGNETS

If I flew parallel to you
The magnets in our wings
May just blow us off our course

Drawn together so
Our planes might crash
This current trajectory
Would not continue
What exists now

Would no longer last

The invisible fabric that binds us

May unravel and pull us
In any number of directions

May even pull us
Apart

The unknown
The unpredictable
Not the safest path
Not the ideal route

Not sure my heart is up for that

So

Let me live far away
Keep our heart energy
Divided by thousands of miles
Chart the safe version
Of our destinies
Protect our legacies

Leave our individual narratives
Separate as they are

Keep our magnetic wings

Apart

142. PARENTS

I had parents
Long ago
Their skin was sun-kissed
Alive and tanned
Smooth under the flesh
Of my small child hands

My father's elbow skin
I used to crinkle
Soft between my fingers
My mother's hair down to her waist
I would twist around my wrist

Their world and their persons
Just extensions of my own
I once felt safest in those arms
The only ones
I had ever known

Now like the girl I once was
That body disappeared
So also now have those two
That version of them
No longer here
Lingering in memory only

Funny how life does that
It gives and it takes away
So much existing in memory alone

In little echo chambers
Little shadows of feeling
Scenes with forever-adjusting lines
Accessed one recollection at a time

I had parents
Long ago
Their skin was sun-kissed
Alive and tanned
And felt smooth under the flesh
Of my small child hands

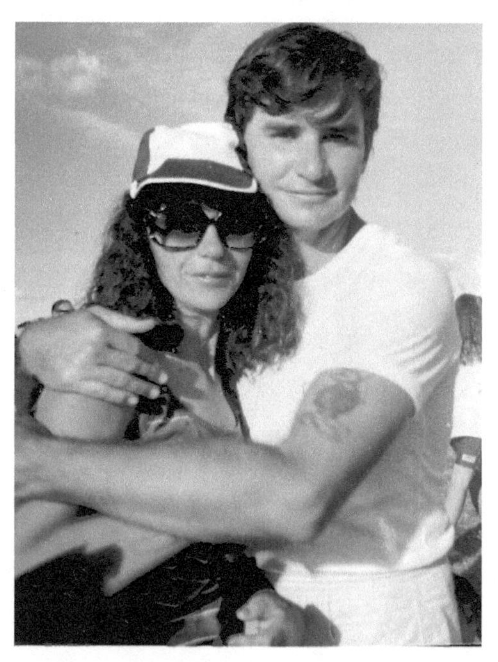

143. THE TRICK

The trick is to be
As thin as paper

Yet as strong as steel

To

Feel
Feel
Feel

And to

Deal
Deal
Deal

To keep your heart
As soft as a cloud

Yet able to flow like a river

To be real

Real
Real
Real

144. A WOLF CALLED HOPE

(A poem given to me in a dream, an ode to hope and new life)

In my dream came to me
The most ragged of beasts
With mange and missing teeth
Limping and in great pain

Yet despite all this
With one steely eye
She looked to me
With great kindness
And the resolve to fight
And see a better day

So I took her in
I gave her milk
And my bed to sleep on
And she began to heal
And then stories to tell
For not an ordinary wolf
Was she

But one very old and ancient
One who has seen
Many a day
One who knew us
Our frailties our foibles
And our weaknesses
As humans

And she said to me

I am Hope
My name is Hope
And it is I
Who gives the future
To all on this earth

But you see
As you have found me

Hope is wearing thin
Hope is wearing out
Hope is slowly dying

For ye all have departed
From the ways of yore
Left your kin
The sky and the sea
Let the waters go sour
Filled the air with poison

Filled your hearts with greed
Greed once a mortal sin
Now greed a celebrated thing

More
More
More

And your hearts are full
Of pride that separates
Friend from friend

No care
No humility
Just me me me

And me

Hope looked at me

Her strength returning
As I fed her bread
And cleaned her coat
And she looked at me
With her eyes of green
Eyes now strong and clear

For we need a new paradigm

One of love and light
And of genuine care
For the healing of all
Depends upon it

Our future depends on it

Hope depends on it

And so I stoked the fire
In that room
Rose myself
Rallied myself
Crossed my heart
Took the lead of the wolf

Swallowed her words

Her health returned
Her radiance glowing
Her teeth like stars
And her eyes like moons

And I inhaled her
And we became one
And we walked through the forest
Followed by crows
And all manner of bird folk

To tell the world
To navigate home
Back to the womb
The womb
Of the mother

The warmth of
The earth

The pillow of hills
The blankets of trees
The living waters
The people
Weary and wild

Returned to each other
Return to the paths
Once well-trod
And the wolf

Again and again

Returned to

The earth and

Returned

To

Me

The people and her

All of us free

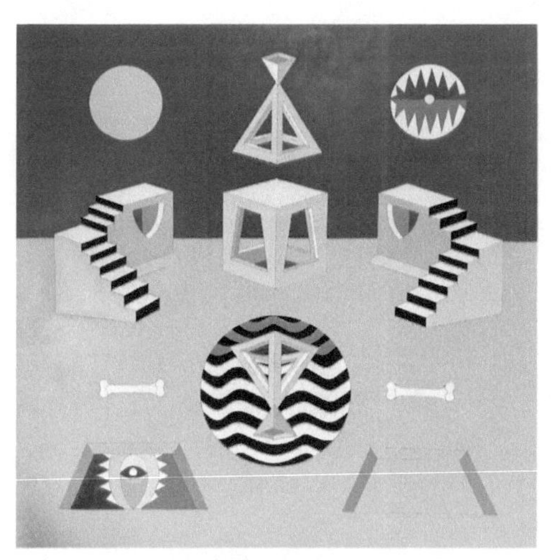

145. SAME SUN (DUALITY OF BEING)

The same Sun that wilts the roses
Burns the hydrangea
Also sends the corn sky high
The pumpkin vine doubles in a day
The tomatoes go
From green to plump red

That same Sun we all rely on
Too much you're done
Not enough
Your fingers freeze

The lesson in that
One to remember

What's good can be bad
What's bad can be good

Tis the measure
And the balance
That is what
Is ever important

Choose carefully then
Where you tread
And how much elixir you consume
What you let yourself inherit

Choose shade
Choose dark

Can't only let the Sunshine shine
We need the black nights too
It is from midnight

That the morning comes

We need polarity
We need duality

So love yourself

In your entirety

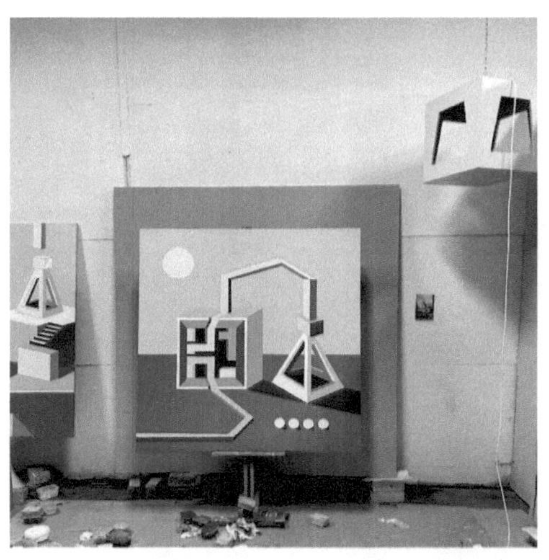

146. QUEEN

Oh Queen
Oh Queen

Can you not see
All your magnificence
Your cup overflowing
With the richest of waters

Unquantifiable
Queen

Your hearth
Your heart
Your breast
Your backbone

All splendid things
Resplendent in
Simplicity
Bones built for
Practicality
Bones built for
Beauty

You who can

Milk your own cow
Dig your own holes
Wherever you please

Make your bed
Lie in it
Fill it with flowers

Choose your life
Every single time

Chose to let
Every skeleton
Fall out of every crack
Every closet
No shame

No one to soothe
Pacify
Or please

Head held high
The Queen of all you desire
Not even a cent spent
Can make you qualify

You with a brood in tow
Or triumphantly solo

Off you go
Off you go

Tears blinding your way
Some days
The sky so terribly gray

But always the blue
Still
Eventually shines
On again through

You who your daughters
Or no daughters
And your sons
Or no sons
And your lovers
Or no lovers
And your friends
All your friends
Will say

She was brave
She braced herself
She was brave

A warrior princess
Then a wise eyed Queen

Her path fortified
Her gates gilded
Her sword
Her bird
And her song

Her heart soft
And yet of stone

Oh Queen
Oh Queen

Do not forget your worth
Do not forget your power
Rise up and claim
All you deserve

All that awaits you
All that you already

Embody

That crown that sits
On your glorious head

Oh Queen
Oh Queen

Unquantifiable

Queen

*Remember you are perfect as you are.
Societal shaping will often have you feeling otherwise.
Allow yourself to find yourself. Your individuality,
the essence of what you have to offer on this earth.
You are aligning with your own power.
Therein lies your greatest potential.

147. ELEPHANTS / LAST WORDS

Can I banish elephants
From the rooms we are in
Reject fake smiles and conversations

Can I tame my own inner circus
And refuse to join
The one around you

Can I feel all I feel
And express all of this
In this moment
And bare my heart honestly

To you

Or is that too much
Too hard to do
Has the moment past
Some truths now left too late

Nowhere to go with them
Only this present left

We are just here
Quietly together
Us and the elephants
Observers of an impossible
Unfathomable
Yet completely human
Situation

I ask myself
Can I return to the beginning
Love that person

Can I be real
Can I be raw
Can I show up
Fully

For this fading version of you
Each and every time
Never knowing which one
Will be the last

Can I not distract myself
Or dissuade myself away
From this hard and terrible thing
Not put my head in the sand

The sandy soft
Comfortable
Warm place of escape

One where you are not dying

So easy to disappear

No I can't

All I can ask really

Is

Please
Please

Give me grace
Give me courage
Give me fortitude

Let this present grief be a power
A clarifying force

So I can be there for you
To kiss your cheek
To honour your journey

To forgive
To accept
You and your life
Your intentions and your limitations

A growing then grown
Now departing human form

Our paths so closely crossed
Your destiny
So paralleling mine

Till now
Till the goodbye
Till the end

Your new beginning
And mine

Our ways parting

Can I be real
Can I be raw
Can I show up

Fully

Fully

Fully

For you

Today
Now and always
Give me grace
Give me courage
Give me fortitude

Let this new grief be a power
A clarifying force
Love conquering all
And let me accept
The elephants in the room

The ones you will take now

Away with you

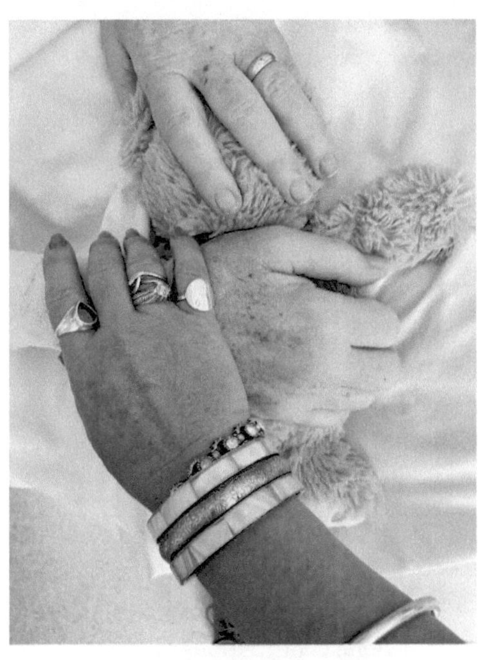

148. CURVEBALLS

All my experiences to date have illuminated this to me, that the curveballs, the difficulties, the griefs and the challenges, these more clearly define and shape our lives than the things we thought we would ourselves choose, the paths we had aspired to follow. That it is the curveballs and the unexpected hard hits that teach us the most. That we can have desires and direction, but that peace, joy and contentment are ultimately found in the surrender to life, as every event is so affected by our perception of it. Not judging things as good or bad but rather as neutral can influence how we deal with them.

A reroute can take you somewhere unplanned, which can deliver greater satisfaction and joy in the bigger picture than what you could ever have imagined for yourself.

You have to trust that things are working out for your highest good.

Even if in the present, it feels like your world is falling apart.

Rarely, a person who has made an impact, or who has gone down in history for achieving anything of note, has had a normal or easy life. Therefore, it can be a helpful perspective to see challenges, loss and grief as a way to find a path to a more grounded, rooted and impactful life.

To whom much is given, much is required. The greater the adversity, the higher the potential to transmute your own difficulties and ways through them into universally helpful contributions to others.

I feel sometimes artists and creatives especially take a hit for the collective conscious. We go through difficult things and then help others, via our work, to make sense of pain and suffering. That we experience loss and hardship and then make and find peace regardless of it, providing a template for others to do the same.

There is a comfort for me in that fact alone. That, via my struggles and the sharing of these experiences, people are better able to resonate with their own. Art opens doorways to feelings. Art connects us all and helps us process our difficult emotions. Try and be curious about the curveballs as they come and look for ways to find a place of calm within them, also ask for divine help. I believe that it is always available to us, and I often feel that it is by the grace of God alone that I am even here.

149. THE ENDLESS Q AND A

I now have far more questions
Than I do answers

Like what if choice has
Little to do with this

What if

Everything is fated
Mapped out
Life predestined

That you and I
Try as we may
Are caught in an
Inescapable maze

Who decides
The when and where

Why are some

People
Places
Things

Forever there

Does love
Or common sense
Or practicality

Have anything
To do with this

Or do souls crash
From one world
To the next

I breathe all this in

This knowing
Wanting
But not wanting

But feeling like
There is no
Steering wheel
No brake

To save us
Them or me

From what may be
The very best
Worst path

From what may be

The love of
This life

And the next life

And

The next

See

Far more questions
Than there are

Answers

150. HOMAGE TO THE MOUNTAINS

I have climbed the Mountains near my home again and again over the last few years. They have become something of a friend and a comfort to me during what has been one of the hardest times of my life. My marriage ended, and a number of people close to me passed away in quick succession.

Climbing the Mountains has felt like a metaphor of sorts, a reminder to not be moved so easily, to return to myself again and again. Every climb reveals something new to me in both the natural world and in my own.

I have laid with my back on the stone peak and have learnt to be quiet enough to feel its ancient vibrations mingle with my own. To be so present that I can feel that. I have cried there, asked all the big questions there, begged for answers there, and been overjoyed and ecstatic there.

While in the Mountains, I have spoken to the wind as though it were all ears. I have sung at the top of my voice. Songs of sorrow and songs of joy. I have stretched out flat in the sun there, absorbing the light. I have been drenched in rain, have been frozen with cold there and yet have felt simultaneously so thrilled to have all my senses feel so alive. When for a long time I felt dead inside.

I have shared my secrets, nursed a breaking heart and yet always, always there is the reminder that like these Mountains I belong to myself, that there is no aloneness when we connect to this belonging deep, deep, down.

While walking, I am reminded again and again to be like these Mountains, to be steadfast, to be grounded, to walk the earth in my own shoes and to tread my own path. To find pleasure in the breeze, in the quiet trees, to find love in the delicate moss, in the patterned craggy rocks, in the tiny wildflowers and in the birds soaring and watching from above. That in the silence of nature, there is love. Love from the purest source. I have learnt to fill my heart with that love.

The Mountains have helped me accept the paradox that is the separateness and the oneness of all things. In this awareness, I have felt a lingering deepened peace. They have helped me care less for many things that I once valued and to appreciate more the simplicity of life. The value of embodying serenity and joy is worth more than gold and material things.

It has also been in the solitude of hiking that I have come to understand that perhaps my biggest calling of all is to share these learnings. That by being vulnerable around my struggles and my discomfort and sharing my ways of navigating forward and through these things, I can support others to do the same.

Know that while there is a sky above, we can always look up. If you can't get to the Mountains, the smallest act of looking up can help on dark days. That we can always lift our eyes and our hearts and ask for more love, and more love, and that this will bring with it all we need for each and every present moment. The present moment is always taking care of the next.

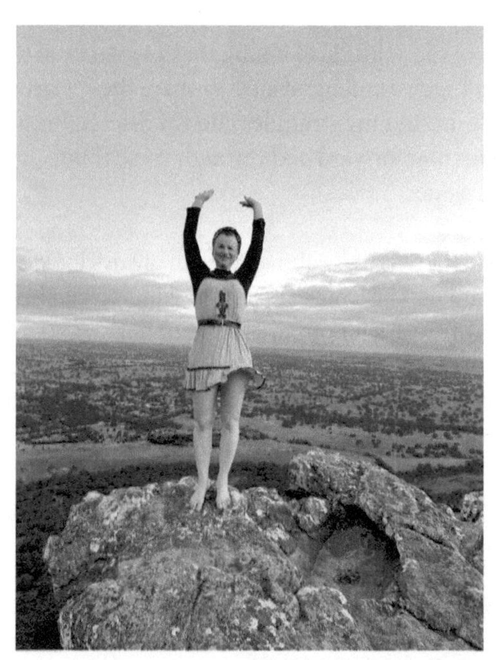

151. MAKING DO

Before I met you
I had to make do
With the Mountains
And this lone
Geological eye
Of mine
As my company

Now I have you
My one eye has become two
I have doubled the scope
Doubled the view

Doubled the heart
Doubled the height
Doubled the love
Doubled my sight

The Mountains and I
We wander with you
No longer alone
No more

Making do

152. MEDICINE

I took the medicine to forget
But it made me remember
Took me back on a journey
Between fate and parallel

Universes

And I remembered you
Remembered your thread
Your planet
Your step

And my eyes widened

At the loss
And the dices rolled
At the chances I took
Everything I overlooked

How I inhaled your smoke

Your smell
Your sweat
I continued

Ignored your warning bell

Ringing anyway
How I sat beside that door
Waiting and yet
Not wanting to be demanding

Preferring to be crucified
Crushed and squashed
Unseen

Ohh what a fool I can be

Out back in my box
Paralyzed and frozen

I took the medicine to forget
But it somehow it
Made me remember

What to never ever
Let myself do

Or be again
Medicine

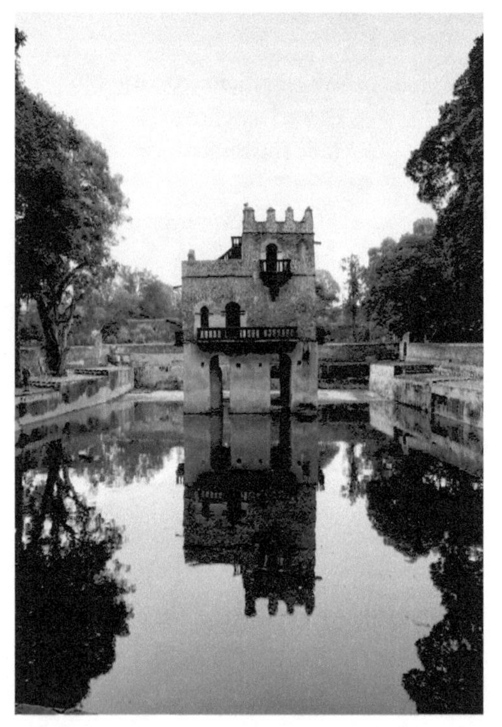

153. SKIN ANGELS REJOICE IN

You and I and angels
Would rejoice
Even now
If your skin
Was to be on mine

Like a song of Solomon
Love and a whisper
These things are blessed
Humanness made divine

We could make rainbows and fireworks
From nothing
But bodies and a bed
Blessed we would ascend

Us being gifted
A lovers pardon
A lovers mantle
For when

You said your heart
Was jammed open
And I should trust fate
Should also open mine

I did

Too wide perhaps
Like my naive eyes
I did not know
How could I foresee

Imagine
What could go wrong

I think of it now

How the mountains
And the seas
Could be dimmed
In value to me

That there could be a love
To squash and diminish all others

Thank you

You and I and angels
Might rejoice

Even now

If your skin
Was to be again

On mine

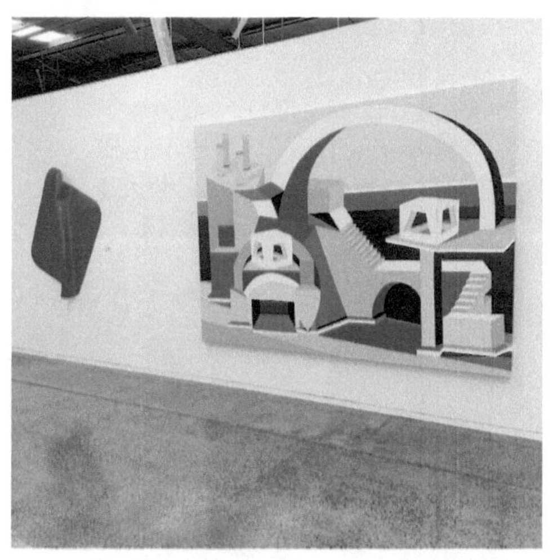

154. LET ME DRINK THE ELIXIR

Love is so foolish
For centuries it's been

Let me drink the elixir
Not fall under the spell

Let me have the magic
Yet be free of loves

Fragility

Is that even possible
How does one protect oneself
From the imminent downfall
But then I let myself be

Lost in you
Given over

Relinquishing control
Letting the heart love

Drinking the elixir
Falling under the spell

Your spell

Your magic

I watch my heart

Fall
Fall

Fell

Watched it be felled
Under your spell

155. FOR MY FATHER

Will the angels call you home tonight

Will the chariot of fire be drawn down

To your bedside

Will your heaving chest be quiet

Will the yellow of your face drain

To pale gray

Will that heart that beat overtime

Be still

Will your breathe become quiet particles

Like dust left in a room

Will time and this place be thick

With the last of you

Will you be here

Tomorrow

Or will tomorrow

You be gone

Energy departed

Energy moved on

Energy gone

But not gone

Farewell my Father

My Father farewell

156. DISAPPEAR

I wanted to curl
Into the smallest of balls and disappear
To take my bleeding heart

And squash it
Squeeze it and clamp it
Stop it feeling
Stop it beating

Stop it

To unwrap my skin from my body
Roll back the tears from my eyes

To
Stop
Stop
Stop

Now to sleep
To leave to somewhere
To dreams
To anywhere
To anyone

But me

Right here
Right now
To disappear

But I don't leave
I hold the pain until it fades
It always does

The pain transmutes to wisdom
Along pathways
It can't travel again

And my heart
Begins to recognise
The comfort of my own

Hand

157. WORN OUT SKIN

The skin of the ocean
From this birds eye view
Flying high above it all
Looks like your dying skin

Unbroken yet swollen
Un burst and tranquil
Full of everything
But life

However

Like the shadow of this plane
Over the sea
The shadow of death
Is hovering over you
And eventually
Over all of us
And over me

Waiting to be set adrift
From a place where
You no longer belong

Like waves bursting banks
Your body is moving on

Your soul soon to follow
Will once again be free

From worn out skin
The song of the ocean
The shadow of the sea

You merge into everything
You merge into nothing
In this way then you do not leave

But forever instead

Your soul

Follows me

158. ICE CREAM

Like ice cream
On a hot tin roof
On the sunniest of days

My love

Slides

Right off

You

Melting
Wasted

Drip by drip

Melted

Done

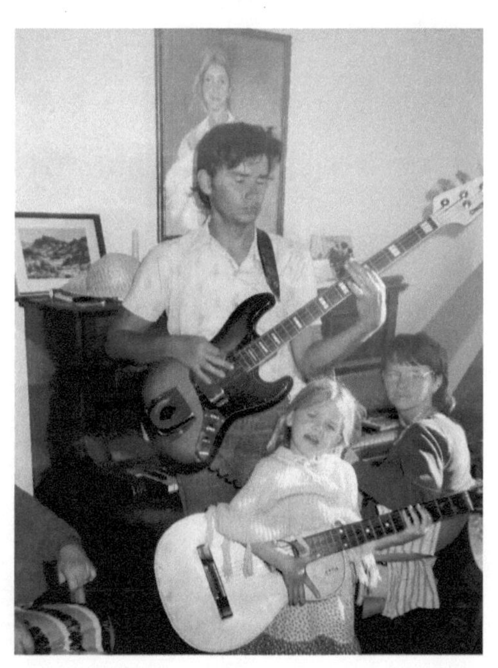

159. JELLY

Like jelly in a string bag
I drip slowly out

Loosing parts of me
I wanted to keep

Memories so deep

My core melting
Diminished

Smaller
Shrunken
Lost

Unable ever again
To be retrieved

At least that is how this feels

Forever altered
My soul lean and tired
My heart
Cracked and leaking

Love and grief

Like jelly in a string bag
I drip slowly out

160. MAGIC MOUNTAIN

Magic Mountain

Climb it with my feet
Climb it in my mind

Magic Mountain

A place within and without
A place both ethereal and eternal

Magic Mountain

Be my guide

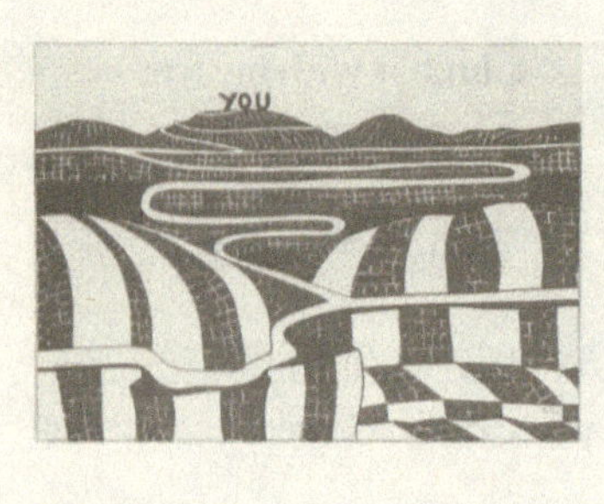
YOU

161. TRIPPING OVER SHADOWS

Tripping over shadows
Flames that never die
Sparks of light on iron
Burning bright and eternal
Reaching for

A blackened sky

Cleanly curling
Twisting turning
Metal never melting
Fire never quelling

Crisping not the silver white

Ner disappearing
Ner disappointing

The body of the soul
Can never die
It's still clean fabric of living
Remains formless
Untouched by the heat of life

Resolute
Smokeless
Ghostlike

Ner disappearing
Ner disappointing

Tripping over shadows
Flames that never die
Sparks of light on iron

Burning bright and eternal
Reaching for

A blackened sky

The body of the soul
Can't be melt
The body of the soul
Can never die

162. SOUL TREES

Like two seeds floating adrift
Miraculously
We found each other
On this same warm shore

A place where the sun shines
Just enough
The light bright and encouraging
And so we grow stretching up and out
Roots intertwined
Branches reaching in all directions
Two idealistic dreamers
Creating a new world around us
New horizons can be seen
From our shared heights
New clouds
For new dreams

And always
The miracle that is
Love
Feeds our shared soil
Feeds our hearts

Keeps us grounded
Planted
Deep

Two seeds
Two trees
One holy

Shared
Connection

One deep
Eternal
Formless
Gifted love

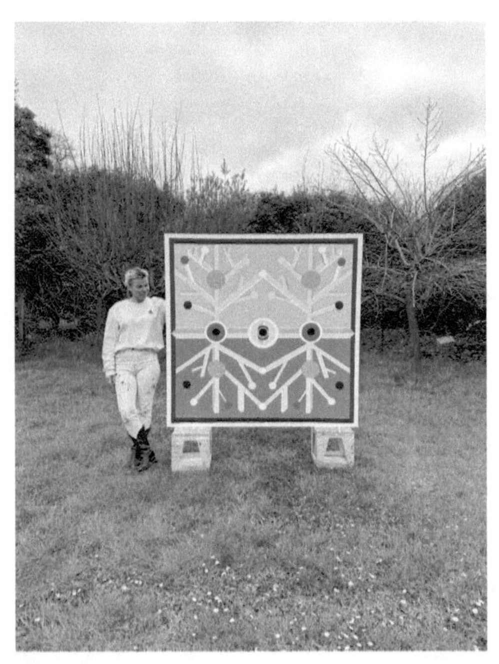

163. WE ARE A NEVER-ENDING STORY

We are a never-ending story
We are more than things
More than body and breath
More than earthly worry
And care

You are divine
Beyond age and time
You are filled full
Of life eternal
Of fire and smoke
From the billion cells
Before you

Do not fear
Transcend this present
You are more than things
More than bone
And flesh and care

Close your eyes
Let your soul remember
Let your heart connect
With the beat
Of the one true thread of life
This one great universe

We are a never-ending story

One stream of love
One river inside

Where nothing is truly lost
And everything is

Waiting

To be found

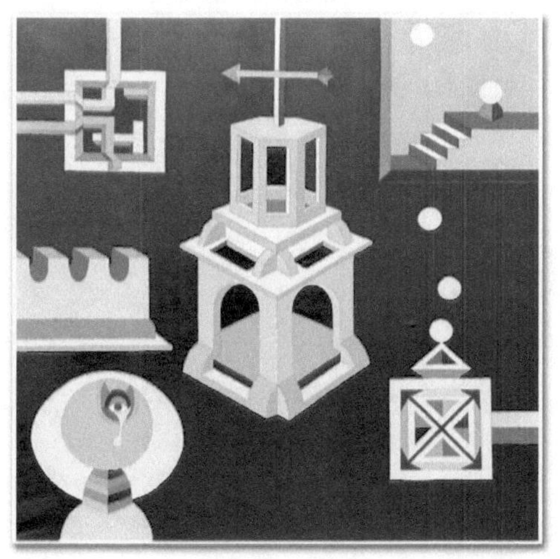

164. WORST KIND OF TIME

I just have to give it time

Let you leak out of my system

Let my blood cool

Let my eyes burn

For new things

New horizons
New shores
New dreams

New mores

Just have to give it time

Bloody heart breaking

Inescapable

Unavoidable

Time

Time of the worst kind

Time that I am

No longer

Yours

And you are

No longer mine

165. KISSING MUD

The stars tipped me up
Shook me out
Head down
Exposed

Ughh

Life is humiliating sometimes
But I can see the reflection
Of gold now
In the mud
Below

When my feet
Are righted

When I am made new
Fresh and ready
Grounded

That will be where
The electricity is

My pockets full
Of new energy

Rerouted me
Reborn via fate and destiny

Things I didn't understand
Did not choose
Did not want

Turning out
To have been
The best for me

Kissing mud

Brought me
Back
To
Me

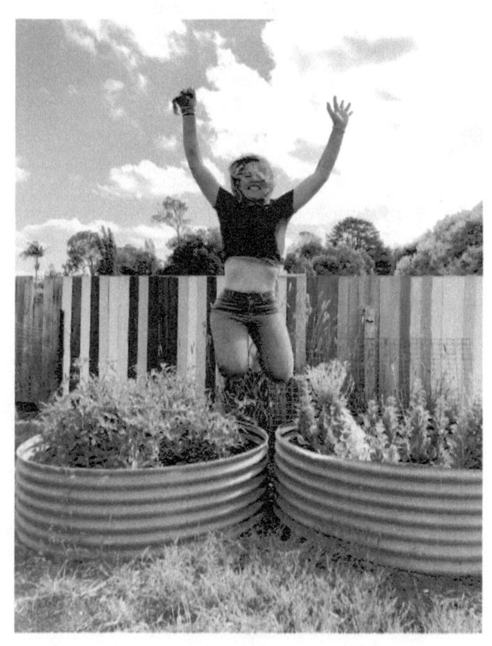

166. LET YOU FLOAT

Ripping up roots
From the soil that was you
So painful
Along with the felling of the tree
Of memories

Shredding of fantasies
Ones that didn't quite fit
Seeing branches crack
Where I once sought safety

My heart attached
So deeply down into the earth
The land of your body
And your cells

Yet like Autumn leaves
Draining my energy
It is time to let you go
So I let you float

Away on the breeze
Our love now dispersed
Scattered like falling seeds
Fragments of hope

On a still forest floor
Where there once was life
There will be again
Life and more

New seasons
New growth
New green

For you
And for me

For as it is in nature
So it is
For all living things

167. BOOK TO PRESS

I did not know you
Until you passed on
Then your life
Had a beginning
And an end
One I could grasp
A thread I could run
My fingers along

Tracing backwards
Winding forwards

Paths that twisted sometimes
But came to wide clearings
The depths of you
Hidden
Came to light
When you left this

Earthside

And then I realised
How deeply
I loved you

How much your presence
Albeit far off comforted me
And now I feel

I know you

You reduced to a wind
In the still summer air
Or a chill up my back
Coinciding with

A thought
You are now a sum of stories
To a body missing flesh
Now I know you
Start to finish

You exist
In my memory alone

You can't add or subtract
From this complete
Memoir

You are done as a book
Gone to press

You are exalted
Because of it

Held high for your charms
Halo covering all
And any wrongs

You are forgiven
Cherished and loved

In this fine version
Of one well lived life

In which

You are so very missed
And so very often

Thought of

168. WALK AWAY

Walk away now
To a place you do not know
Take your past and leave it
In there

Put it in the creek
Let it in on flow
Flowing on down
To the river

Let it rush into the sea
Away from me
Then we will see
If there is somewhere
Love can go

Pictures of the past
You can't leave behind
Kiss goodbye
They were yesterday

Put them in a tree
The wind will set them free

They will fly away
Around and around
Forever

Let them blow
You will be free
Free to love me
I am sure we will find somewhere
This love can go

Walk away
Let it all on away

Flow Flow Flow

Walk away
Let it all in on away

Blow Blow Blow

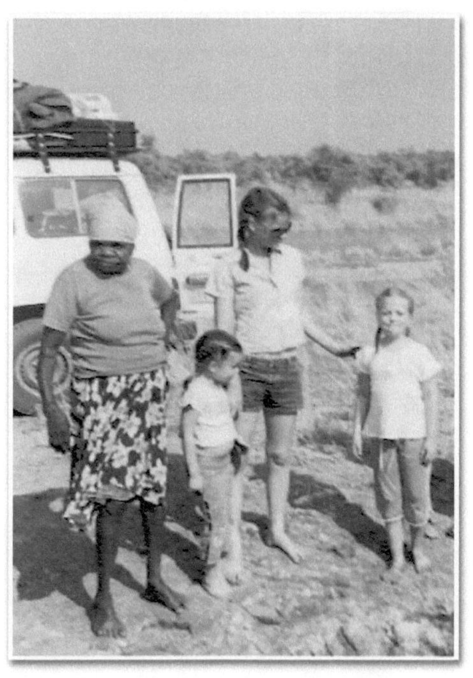

169. SANDMAN

I think the sandman died
Too many tears I've cried
I'm long over being mad

Left with just being sad

Sleeps eluded me again
Nothing here my friend
My heart left the space it had
A prison a cage

But a choice
I made

Restless waiting for the dawn
New day new life heart torn
Between the past and that pain
And the future

Wide awake I am

I tell myself to look within
That courage is but a breath away
So weary my eyes have been
But no more a fool of life

I'll be

A foot placed right now is a step forwards
And no insomnia and grief
Can hold me
Where I used to be

Sleep eluded me again
But I lie awake making plans
My heart is alive and free
No prison no cage

Just a choice I made

For me

170. TILL IT RAINS

*For my parents who the NT forever changed, they left their bones there

Be careful who you send
Into the dry lands
You gird them up
And then you let them go

Choose wisely who is sent
To save the dead men
Look for character
Iron will and backbone

For

Their tears will fall
For the misery they feel
Their offspring will leave
And wander off

At will

Their life blood bogged
They cannot turn the wheel

Dry dead land
Drinks life and will drink till

Till eventually it rains
And the storms will split the sky
And a fleeting freedom
Finally comes

And with the rain the pain
Is temporarily
Washed away

Tears they come
There will be no shame
Everything made new

Again

Or so they say

But

Then the momentary reprieve
Is done

And everything is burning again
Rain dried out
Like a quick fix drug
Reality is back

Once again
Bent over weary with the day
Sun beats down relentless
In its task

When will this be over
I hear you say
God when will we see some mercy
You ask

In a trance it seems
The days are slipping by

And an overall apathy
Has settled into the bones

And the feeling takes away
Even the urge to cry

And everyday is just consumed
With doing
What needs to be done
Barely surviving
Under this endless
Never ceasing
Sun

Be careful who you send
Into the dry lands
The dead men might just

Keep their bones

171. SEASONS END

Leaves all a blowing
Long grass all drying
It was this time last year
It all ended

And the cold air reminds me
Of the things we said
As the wind blew away
With our dreams

I woke up with eyes
Sore from crying
Reality hitting me again
Our love was long gone

Dry like dry red dirt
I could not find a reason
To stay on one hand

And over and over
I replay the scenes

And over and over
It turns out the same

I am wondering
Over and over

Again

How love can end up
Being pain

Yet so the seasons
Will go on by
Spring turns to rain

Goes back round to dry

A scar to remind me
Of wounds that have healed
I will probably have fallen

In love again

And over and over
I replay the scenes
And over and over
It turns out the same

I am wondering

Over and over

Again

How love can end up

Being pain

And a memory

That fades

And decays

172. HEART AND HOUSE

Kept my doors locked
Heart and house
You turned up
And turned a magic key

So I let you in

In spite of me

Heart aching for too long
House home all alone
Bright star in a blackened sky
There you were

So I let you in

In spite of me

Here you are with an angel's face
This house no more needing space
My tears somehow
Evaporate

I let you in

In spite of me

Gave you all my keys
Opened all my doors
From the cellar set myself free
Let you love me

Let you in

In spite of me

173. FORK IN THE ROAD

You can forget your dreams
You can forget being free
You can forget respect
You can forget loving me

The way you are walking
Further into the dark
The road it won't get shorter
Present won't be past

Too far gone
You may lose your way
Never to return
What are you going to do

A fork in the road

What are you going to choose

This path of self destruction
You are currently on
You can expect retribution
You can expect to feel pain
You can expect disappointment
You can expect
To live in vain

You will try to retrieve what is lost
You will wish at any cost
You will wish a different choice you made
You will want
Your past to trade

You can live without a conscience
You can live like you won't pay
You can live like there is no tomorrow
You can live for yesterday

Please choose life
Please choose love

Please choose
Me

174. ORIGAMI

We are folded like origami

One into the other

Like paper though

We too are only temporary

Bodies seeking heat

Warmth and love

In this season of winter

In this mutual cold

While we both await

A summer day to dawn

I unfold

I uncurl

I flatten

I take myself home

My heart full

My back remembering

Softened not creased

Lines made for

Human

Origami

175. INERTIA

Is inertia on our side
Or are we victims to it
This pull
This snowball rushing
Down a hill
This new chemistry
This exploration
This intention
It is inertia
Carrying blood now
To new extremities
This momentum
Carrying us down
A Mountain side

Too hard to pull up
Too fast to
Slow it down
It was always
On its way
Threads overlapping
Invisible for so long
Now seen
Magic from its birth
An energy
We are testing
Its force
Too fast
Too slow
Defying time
Is inertia on our side
Could we walk away
Or are we victims
To its fate
No answer to be found
We submit
To its holy
Its mutual
Its sacred
And solemn
Ground

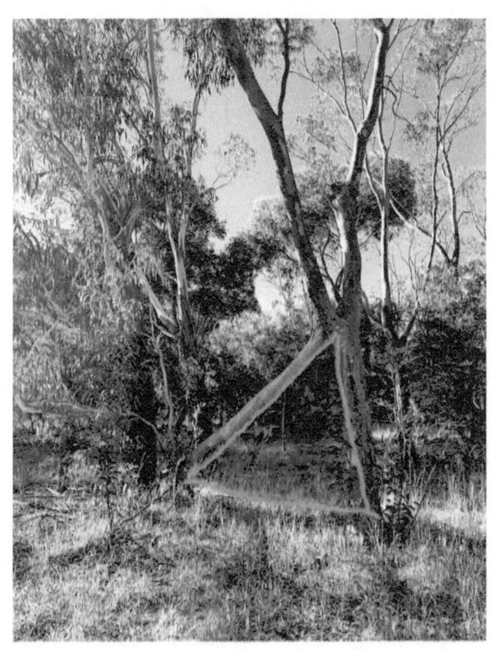

176. WE SWALLOW THE SKY

As rock returns to mountain
And rivers run to the atmosphere
The heart returns to itself
Once broken

In time it becomes
Whole again

But that space in between
With heart in a groundless mouth
This is where we learn
What it is to be human

To be mortal
The difference between flesh and stone
You will never be the same

Never the same

Yet

Stronger along the lines
All was torn
You were torn

You can only be one
You can never be separated
You will be ok

You cannot lose yourself here
You are safe
Within the home that is

You

Do not fear the brokenness
Do not fear the world within
And around you ending
It has always been this way

We live eternal
Yet we lose form
We always have
We always will

Trust in
The recalibration
Of blood and memory
Of past and future

In this present
We like all other elements
Make order from chaos

The material existence
Of which we are one and the same
We also exist governed by these laws
So we return to substance

Like water to a well

So again I say
Do not fear the fall

There is always a landing
Always a circle
Dust to dust
A timeless proverb

Nothing is new

No agony no loss
Be comforted by this
For tis in all our endings
That beginnings are begun

May your cells be held
In this rent of time
By this knowledge

Nothing is ever complete
To stars we rise and run
And in every day
Breath by breath

We slowly swallow the sky

177. LOVE VS FEAR

LOVE EXPANDS
MULTIPLIES
REJOICES

JEALOUSY AND HATE
SHRINK AND CONTRACT
AND ARE ROOTED
IN FEAR
AND IN LACK

IF ONE ALLOWS THEMSELVES
TO BE A CUP
FULL OF LOVE

THERE IS LITTLE ROOM
FOR ANYTHING ELSE

FOR LOVE WILL ALWAYS BE

THE FAR GREATER

FORCE

178. SLIDING DOORS / SHIFTING WALLS

Places we meet
Chances we take
Roads that lead

To one destination

Sliding doors
Shifting walls

Time overlapping
Hearts mending
And breaking
And mending

Again

A room called fate
A place called destiny
A time called

Se - ren - dip - ity

Where all good things start
Where all good things end

This is us
This is where
We are at

This is where
We end

And where
We begin

179. I FOLLOWED THE WIZARD HOME

I followed the Wizard home
Down the Mountain side
The sandy path aglow
Lit by full moonlight

A shock of white on white
Against a foreign sky
Our feet finding their way
Barefoot and unafraid

My heart held up high
A compass in the night
With fate and faith a plenty
We too shall soon arrive

I followed the Wizard home
Down the Mountain side
The sandy path aglow
And lit by full moonlight

I followed the Wizard home

180. HERE I AM

Landed
Grounded
Outside or inside
Often I can't tell

Could I squeeze
Through the eye
Of a needle

Could I change
Adapt
Adjust

Go somewhere
I do not belong
Just to be loved

No that was before

So

Here I am
Landed
Grounded
Inside and outside

Here where the love is

Here where I belong

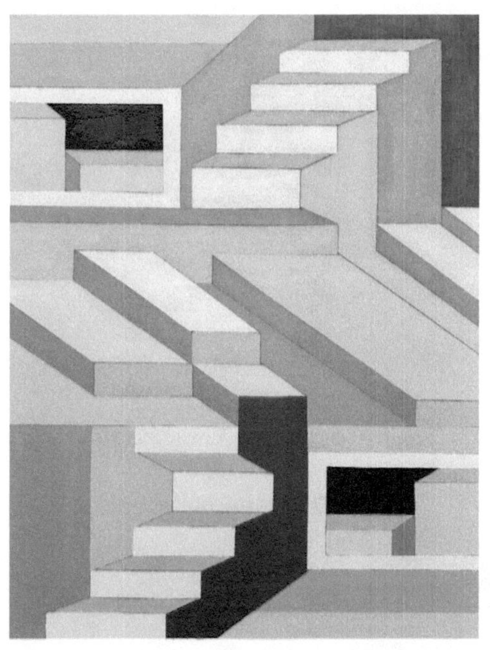

181. YOUR FACE UNDER MY LIDS

Do I then just
Never go to bed again
Do I never shut my eyes
Risk seeing your face
Under my lids
In my dreams

Your face
And all the faces
I have ever loved
And lost
Simultaneously
Looking back at me
Breaking my heart
The absence too much

Do I swim to the depths
Of the ocean
The blackness
Enveloping my entire being

Do I fall from the highest peak
And let the bliss of wind
Catch me
Or catch me not

This this this

Blanket of me
I cannot leave
All the feelings
Wrapped around me
Always anymore

Like shards of glass
Or feathers of love
Or misery or joy
Or fallen seeded stars
The blanket of humanity
Of body
Of soul

Like a prayer
An echo
A noise so loud
It becomes silence

This is it
This is all

Eventually the longest sleep
Of all comes

The rest of the gods
The rest of the titans
The bones stacked

Where we leave them

And no dreams
Or deep sea
Or mountain breeze
Or blanket of stars or soot
Can cover me

And finally
I am free

Free
Free

182. THE DRAGON AWAKES

The Dragon said
Lay down your breast plate
That piece that covers your heart
Your sword sits by your side
Take off your shoes

Rest

The war is over
The fight is done
Here in the soft sand
Under a setting

Sun

You can take shelter
Drink the clear water
Lay your head
On the chest of another

Have the sweat kissed
From your brow
The war is over
The fight is done

The Dragon said
Take up the stone
The one with the fire inside
Let it guide you now
Let loves light take you

Home

No need for armor
No need for cover
The Moon now above you
The darkness now ever a glow

The Dragon lit blood
Fresh in your veins
The old forest burnt now
Behind you

The strength once only
In your armor
Replaced now
By your fortified

Bones

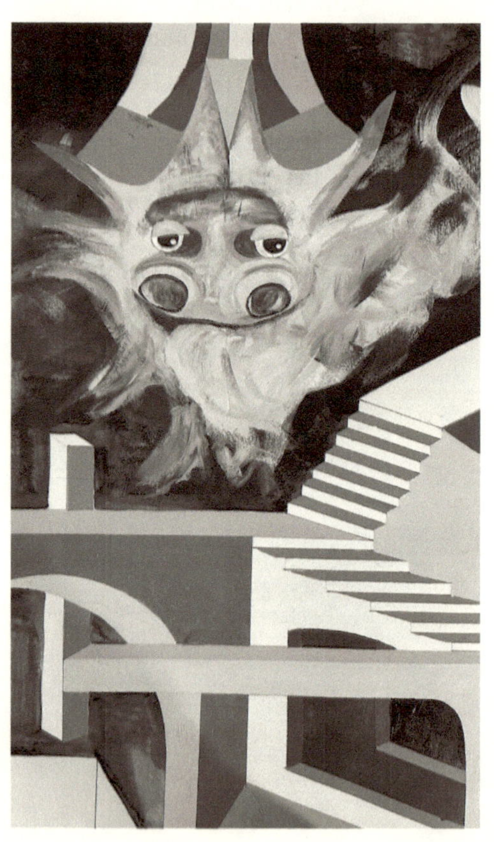

183. BELLS

Bell as center

As womb
As mother
As intuition
As lover

Bell as voice
Bell as vibration
Bell as silence
Bell as wound

Bell as celebration
Bell as loss
Bell as heart torn
Bell as babies born
Bell of grief
Bell of joy

Bell for you
Bell for me
Bell for us

Bell of eternity

Bell as Mountain
Bell as tower
Bell as spirit
Bell as soul

Bell of beginnings

Bell of ends

Bell of now
Bell of never

Bell as center

184. WAITING FOR ME

I feel like a ship
Departing from your shore
Like Lot's wife looking back
Like Colombus searching for more
Another homeland
Like Frida
Heart hurting more than body

My cells wide
As the infinite ocean
Seeking out yours
And finally
Drawing a tide
With no landing shore

Like an angel
With wings exhausted
Letting them hang
Closed for a time
Like a dreamer waking mid scene
Who cannot find
A feel-good ending
Like a bee in a desert of sand
Its eternal flower lost

This is reality
And this is me

Waiting in my field of nothing
Waiting for you

But mostly
Waiting for me
To return to the me

Without

You

185. FINGERS OF THE GODS

Can we play with fire and light

Fingers full like
Torches of the gods
We create sparks with bodies
With desires looks and thoughts

We are once born current
We are human lightning bolts
We ignite life minute by minute
Masses of beautiful shiny cells

We once looked for this light
In the blackened skies above

Yet from our bellies
Our centre and our middle
That's where it's long been from

So can we play with fire and light

Let our hearts be bravely lit
Beam light into the darkness
Be struck like matches
Again
And again
And again

To be vessels seeking alchemy
Transformation and transmutation
You and me for eons and infinity
To burn and not be burnt

To be all we are yearning to be

To play with fire and light

To play with fire and light

Play with fire and light

186. MEDICINE FOR A BROKEN HEART

Slow down
Put your hand on your heart
Wrap the other arm around yourself
You were born in this body
This place is your home
Return to it
Hold yourself
Think about the ways
You can care for it
To forgive it
To be compassionate towards it
To invest in it
Broken hearts take time to heal

Like broken bones
Broken hearts
We need to rest
Need tending to
Feed yourself nourishing things
Sleep in
Treat yourself like a patient
As best you can
Hearts need the same
The same care and attention
As other bodily pains
You will not always feel this way
Even though in this present
It feels this way
Like other hurts
This one too will pass
Eventually
Let the intensity burn through you
For a time
There is a balance to find
Do not wallow in it
But do not bury it
To have to revisit it
Another time
Take your pain out day by day
Take yourself out
Take yourself home
Cry when you need to
Give it full attention
Then give it no attention
Find beauties to distract you
In the clouds
And in the flowers
In animals
Friends and other static
Small joys

And at some point
You will
Have more good moments
Than bad
You will be ok
You will be stronger in time
You will be wiser somehow
Will have learnt something
Remember
There is no new human loss
Your will feel like you again
One day
You will love again
Your broken heart
Will be whole again
Return to you now
To your life
Dig up your dreams
Hold yourself
The only thing
That remains

187. THE PEARL

Back to the center
To the heart
To thine own arms
To thine own soul

The beauty
And the terror
The darkness
The weight
The pressure

Is what makes

A pearl

In the murky depths
A luminous light
Is formed

188. THIS ETHEREAL ARCHITECTURE

This ethereal architecture
The scaffolding of mind
Bridging time and space
Transcending materiality
Pared back to exist only
In the bones of nature
Attached to the sands of time
To the whispering of trees
To the blood of you and me
Weaving a fabric unseen
Threading cosmos to core
Looping invisible
Around Mountains
Back to the center
Back to a middle
Twisting and bending
Gridding unruly seas
Sweeping invisible magic
Around you and around me
Around the forests
Around the fallen
Around the lost
It is the quiet bedrock of the soul
The translucent net
It is what separates

The lucid waking dream
From physical reality
This ethereal architecture
Connecting earthly frames
To ancestral long-gone places
Holding humanity in its entirety
Geometric materiality
The magic
The utopia
The fantasy
The narrative trapped
In this
Ethereal architecture
Acknowledging
The time that the sky fell
And that the waters have swelled
Stories soil and stone can tell
This ethereal architecture
This world of its own
That remains to pay homage
To the past
And hold a mirror of clues
Ringing subconscious bells
Illuminating what exists to be seen
By the eyes open to seeing
The ethereal architecture
The atmosphere that surrounds
Envelopes and holds us
Bringing life to the living
Ever present
Always in waiting
Present in air
Always here
Always there
Holding light
Holding flame

This ethereal architecture
The scaffolding of mind
Bridging time and space
Transcending materiality

Transcending the mind
Of you and of me
For now
And for all time

This ethereal architecture
This gap
Between your heart

And mine

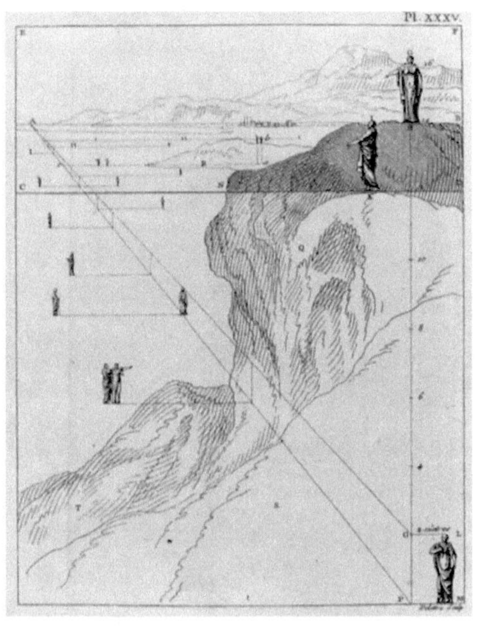
Pl. XXXV.

189. SURRENDER OF BODY TO PLACE

In the surrender
Of my body

To a place
To a center

I render my mind to grounding
The electricity once dispersed

Is homed

I am recalibrated
Again
And again
Like an ancient being
The Mountain and I

Have not aged

Here too I am timeless
Alive in the middle of art and science
Ideas transmuted

Cleanly
Evenly
Distributed

Like lovers giving in to
Unceasing desire
Like a magnificent
Dying tree felled
Like a dam bursting
With winter rain
Like a racing forest fire

It was always inevitable

Always
This

The surrender of a body

To a place
To a middle
To a center
To time

The surrender of body to place
The surrender of me

To you

190. REALITY

Perception creates reality
This being a powerful fact
Henry Thoreau said
It is not what you look at
But what you see
And it is true
What you give your energy
And your attention to
You get more of
Your attitude determines
Your altitude
Two people
Same circumstances
Different outcome
Different perceptions

When look back on my life
I can see
How my choices to move
Through and forward
Have changed everything
To focus on what I have
What is in my hand
Over my lack
Or disadvantage
How this has profoundly shaped
This present and wonderful
Creative reality
My encouragement to you
Start where you are
With what you have
Challenge your limitations
Your mindset
What you feel to be true
Expand on that
Dream the dream
And daily do one thing
Towards that
Be mindful of what you look at
And what you choose to see
For you second by second
Create your own

Reality

191. KILLING COSMIC DARLINGS

I once created a body of work derived from the literary term *kill your darlings*, meaning to kill off excess in the written form. To consider what is important and then to ruthlessly trim back. Words, characters and anything else no longer serving the core storyline or plot must go.

I thought about this in the broader context of life itself and how every now and then it is necessary to do the same. To consider even the aspects of self and the ways of being you may have come to love and are attached to under a microscope and to then in a large scale, broad sweep, let what no longer serves you go. It requires a cosmic effort to push against the inertia that underpins the day to day and to change. To let go, to burn away, to move forward. Often, we only do this when our lives force this action upon us in some way via some catastrophe, event or breakdown of life as we know it.

I then thought of this concept and how it also applies to a creative life. How we can so often fall into familiar and comfortable ways of working and staying within safe an expected parameters. Yet, how counter to true creative expression this actually is, that in order to not stagnant you have to sacrifice the familiar and predictable patterns. Push yourself out of your comfort zone artistically, for it is in this space of not knowing that the "magic" happens. Here you get that fail or flush adrenaline happening and new ideas and inspiration can flood through.

So, this has been part of my journey, considering not only the aspects of my personal life that don't serve me, but my creative life as well. Allowing myself to explore new figurative and other elements and fresh ways of storytelling within my paintings and my practice overall. I am curious to see what will unfold as a result of this and anticipate new and good things to come.

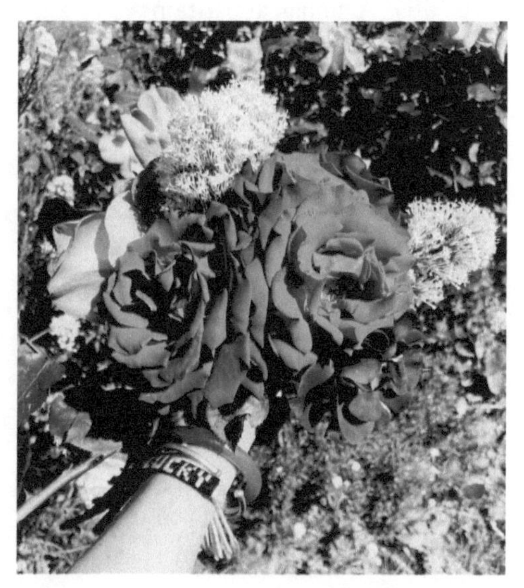

192. IF LIFE WERE A MOVIE

Under a dramatic backdrop
Inky blue sky
Luminous blood Moon
On a white sandy path

I saw you

Some kind of sign
A human apparition
You arrived unexpectedly
A brand-new character

And if my life were a movie
If it was a stage with many acts
I am at peace with that

For all that came before you
All I learnt the hard way
Has allowed me

To see you

To understand you
It led me to you

So now

A grand new stage
A fresh beginning
A brand-new film
An unscripted part

If life were a movie
Then this is that scene

When everything
In a dramatic plot twist

Has somehow finally

Fabulously and magically

Worked out

IN CLOSING

I have had so much love, been gifted with five incredible children, yet have also had so much loss, so many changes and really so many mini lives packed in. I feel 100, I feel 10, I feel translucent, I feel like stone. So many contradictions. I also can't help but feel that the best is yet to come, That life holds even more of the good I have experienced so far.

For all the experiences I am ultimately profoundly grateful. Everything a lesson, even the worst of things held the gift of a new understanding. Every grief has shown me a door to an expansion, every joy has stuck in my cells as a kind of cushion to the knocks. I have been brave when my back was against a wall, I am an artist because of this resilience.

This morning, I am not sure again of where the path ahead lies. I am often uncertain, except for the old worn and comfortable predictability of showing up to paint, to love my kids, to disappear into a daydream, to put one foot in front of the other again and again. Every step leading to the here and now, to this version of life. Every decision a micro-decision towards some new reality. Showing up with a big heart and openness and hoping I am getting it right.

I am sharing this collection of contrasts as I know am not alone in grappling with the wildness of the journey at times. The desire to not be human, yet at the same time the luxury and the privilege that it is to be so.

Looking back reminds me I can do hard things, to draw on the wisdom of those ahead of me, that the best is yet to come. That my gift is to see the opportunity in every adversity. To transmute difficulty into lived experience, helping me lift those who need me at any given point.

That the journey has led me to this point of peace, that I could not be here without there.

Also, acknowledging all the beautiful people on my path, for friends who have been family and to everyone who has supported me over the years. Impossible to briefly sum up. Most of you will find yourself somewhere in my work.

Out of words for now...

Jasmine X

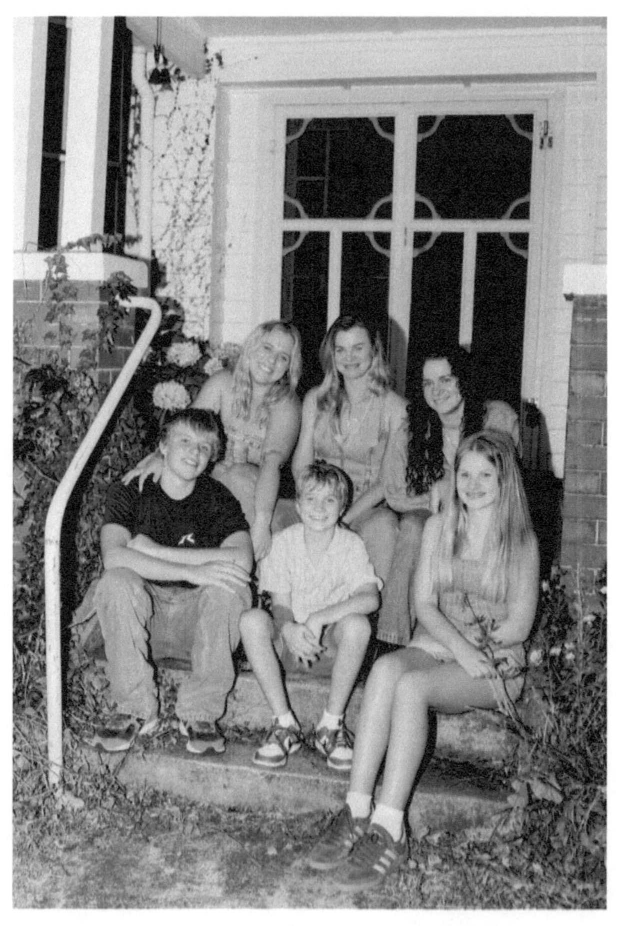

IMAGES INDEX

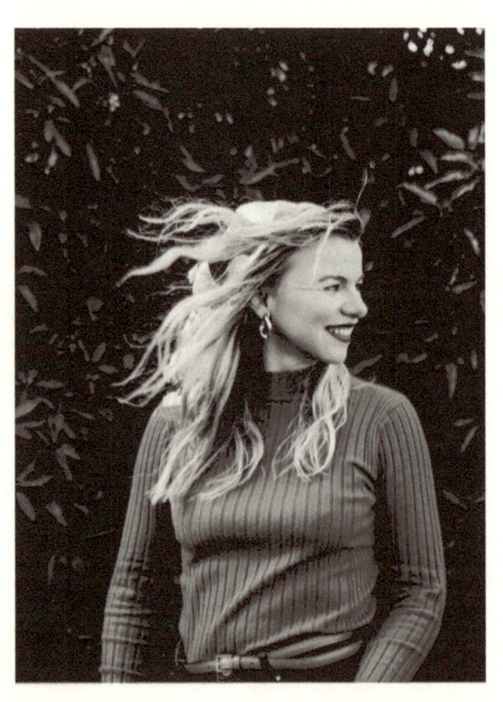

ABOUT THE AUTHOR

Jasmine Mansbridge is an Australian multidisciplinary artist and writer whose work blends architectural form, symbolic language, and philosophical inquiry to explore the human experience. A self-taught artist, she began painting at the age of seventeen while living in the remote town of Katherine in the Northern Territory. Living closely with Aboriginal artists and communities deeply shaped her symbolic and narrative approach. This foundation continues to influence her work today.

Now based in the Grampians in regional Victoria, Jasmine is a mother of five and a full-time artist working across painting, sculpture, installation, public art, digital animation, poetry, and film. Her visual language is grounded in geometry and metaphysical symbolism, with recurring motifs such as cubes, pyramids, portals, and gazebos acting as vessels for thought, reflection, and transformation. These forms invite viewers to consider the structure of both their inner and outer worlds.

Her work has been exhibited internationally, with solo exhibitions and commissioned projects in New York, Beijing, Hong Kong, London, Melbourne, and Sydney. She has created large-scale public works, immersive installations, and collaborations that incorporate augmented reality, architecture, and storytelling. Jasmine has also participated in international art residencies and received professional development grants that support the ongoing evolution of her creative practice.

Inspired by sacred geometry, spirituality, mythology, architecture, and the rhythm of domestic life, Jasmine creates from a place of curiosity and quiet discipline. Through paint or poetry, she invites stillness, offering contemplative moments that quiet the noise of daily life.

International curator and arts commentator Carrie Scott, of Seen London, has described Jasmine's work in the following terms:

"Mansbridge's work bridges the tangible and the metaphysical, transforming complex ideas about identity, connection, and existence into striking visual forms. Her practice, rooted in the traditions of Neo-geo art, draws on the precise geometry of minimalism, the boldness of pop art, and the illusionistic depth of op art. These influences, combined with a deeply personal exploration of spirituality, result in work that feels both intimate and universal.

At its core, Jasmine's art is about navigating the spaces between — between the self and the world, the physical and the spiritual, humanity and nature. Her meticulously crafted sculptures, installations, and paintings serve as portals, inviting viewers to reflect on their place in the cosmos and the barriers, both internal and external, that shape their reality. She doesn't just depict; she disrupts, asking us to confront what we hold onto and what we need to let go of to move through the world more freely.

While her work feels surreal and otherworldly, it is grounded in deeply human concerns: the search for meaning, the desire to connect, and the challenge of change. Jasmine's practice is about recalibration — reminding us of our estrangement from nature and offering a pathway back to harmony. Her pieces are not just visual statements but tools for contemplation, encouraging us to pause, reflect, and ultimately reimagine the way we engage with the world and with ourselves."
— *Carrie Scott, Curator / Seen London*

To learn more about Jasmine's work and creative journey,
visit: *www.jasminemansbridge.com*